The Spokesman

AF234591

Trident –
Nuclear Proliferation the British Way

Edited by Ken Coates

**Published by Spokesman for the
Bertrand Russell Peace Foundation**

Spokesman 98   **2008**

CONTENTS

Editorial   **3**   *Ken Coates*

Is a Nuclear-Weapons-Free   **7**   *Maj Britt Theorin*
World Achievable?

Nuclear Disarmament –   **17**   *Mayors for Peace*
Still Waiting

The Cost of Nukes   **21**   *Jackie Cabasso*

Conversion Currency   **24**   *Alexis Lykiard*

Willie and Maud   **27**   *Trevor Griffiths*

Reviews 94
Direct Democracy   *Achin Vanaik*
Recent Times   *Abi Rhodes*
How Did David Kelly Die?   *Michael Barratt Brown*
Pioneer   *Stan Newens*
Criminal Folly   *MBB*

Subscriptions
Institutions £35.00
Individuals £20.00 (UK)
£25.00 (ex UK)

Back issues available on
request

A CIP catalogue record
for this book is available
from the British Library

Published by the
Bertrand Russell Peace
Foundation Ltd.,
Russell House
Bulwell Lane
Nottingham NG6 0BT
England
Tel. 0115 9784504
email:
elfeuro@compuserve.com
www.spokesmanbooks.com
www.russfound.org

With thanks to Steve Bell
Printed by the Russell Press Ltd., Nottingham, UK
ISSN 1367 7748   ISBN 978 0 85124 751 9

Editorial

Trident – Nuclear Proliferation the British Way

Back in 1984, at a time when the British Labour Party policy favoured European Nuclear Disarmament, Gordon Brown declared that the Trident programme was 'unacceptably expensive, economically wasteful and militarily unsound'. In those far off days the Labour Party favoured the simultaneous dissolution of the North Atlantic Treaty and the Warsaw Pact.

Gingerly feeling its way, the Kinnock leadership gradually accomplished the retreat from unilateralism, at the very time that true multilateralism had become a possibility. The Warsaw Treaty demobilised itself and went home. Its East European members severed their connections with the Soviet Union, which itself disintegrated, losing the Baltic States, parts of the Caucasus, and considerable influence in Central Asia. For Russia, these areas became part of the 'near abroad' which gave rise to the need for complex diplomacy and a considerable effort to influence other alignments. As Russia generated privatisation, oligarchs, and confusion on a grand scale, all the paradigms of deterrence were evacuated of whatever meaning they might once have held.

But in Britain, the Trident programme went on and on. Britain's only system of nuclear armaments had been furnished by the United States, which provided the ballistic missiles direct, and also the blueprints of the submarines themselves as well as of the warheads, together with a not inconsiderable volume of technical assistance in their construction. The missiles themselves are purebred red-blooded American armaments in every detail. Fifty-eight of them are leased on rotation by the British Government and deployed on four Vanguard submarines. They apparently also figure in the calculations of the Americans themselves about their overall deployment. Various failsafe mechanisms prevent stray missiles from launching themselves against anywhere in the world where the Americans do not wish them to go.

Of course, the main failsafe device is an embarrassingly subordinate and totally compliant British Government. This has long since lost any pretensions to independence and sees its defence policy as necessarily anchored in every detail to the needs of Washington.

The United States entered the new millennium with a rigid commitment to 'full spectrum dominance' in all military matters. Top dog: that was where the U.S. of A. was at. This managed to shrink other commitments almost to the point of invisibility. True, the Nuclear Non-Proliferation Treaty survived, but since the world's megapower was determined to interpret this entirely selectively, it was unlikely to create problems. It would be useful in restricting the nuclear options of rogue or dubious States, but it could be instantly set aside in the case of putative allies. It never caused the slightest problems for Israel, perhaps the most serious proliferator in the most dangerous zone of the world, and it created only momentary difficulties for India and Pakistan.

But over time America's wars have sapped American hegemony. Timid signs of life have even been observed in the United Nations. It is no longer axiomatic that world diplomacy must follow the script written in the State Department.

What, in this context, happens to the doctrine of deterrence? This doctrine was clearly much cited in relations between East and West, in the days before the implosion of the Soviet Union. Did it ever apply in other regions, such as the Middle East? It is difficult to disentangle appearances from realities in this region. The Bush/Blair alliance strayed into the battlefield in order to suppress weapons of mass destruction that did not exist in Iraq. That made the task of suppression all the easier.

The same intelligence services which got things so dramatically wrong in that country have intermittently played up the dangers of nuclear weapons in Iran. But these too, it appears, are fictitious. According to most conventional doctrines of deterrence, the Iranians need nuclear weapons in order to inhibit possible attacks by Israel, which has already demonstrated not only its willingness, but also its competence, to assume the role of nuclear policeman by attacking and destroying the Osirak reactor in Iraq in 1981.

If Israel's responses were confined to belligerent rhetoric, it might be pardonable to dismiss the Israeli threat to neighbouring States. But there is a rather large record of painful military adventures which breeds fierce agnosticism on this score.

The Iranians are also hemmed about by other nuclear neighbours in India and Pakistan. In Western folklore India is a 'good' nation which cannot nourish militaristic expectations. That is as may be. But not many people will stand up to proclaim similarly benign interpretations of Pakistani policy, and there may indeed be doubt about whether the proprietors of the Pakistani deterrent will remain securely in place for very long. Senator Obama has let it be known that if the Pakistani bomb falls into the wrong hands, he would favour military action to 'recover control'. Were there any truth at all in the deterrence theory, the bomb in Pakistan would surely constitute a big enough threat, and a large enough uncertainty, to justify the speediest possible counter-deployment. But instead, and mercifully for all of us, the official Iranian reaction is to renounce any intentions of pursuing nuclear armaments. Not only does Iran repudiate the bomb, but her supreme leader pronounced a fatwa against it.

There is only one rational antidote to all those free range bombs, in the hands of all those temperamental and unstable leaders: and it is indeed the renunciation of nuclear weapons and the establishment of a nuclear-free zone in the entire Middle Eastern region. Difficult though this may be to achieve, its advantage over the alternative of frenzied preparation for nuclear mayhem all around the zone, is perfectly obvious to all but the proprietors of full spectrum dominance and military orthodoxy.

All of this argues that perhaps the most useful weapon in the UN armoury might be the Non-Proliferation Treaty, and the doctrine of nuclear-free zones. But the British Government, whose international doctrine is thick with pieties about the United Nations, is totally indifferent to this key institution.

We already drew attention to this (*Spokesman No. 92*), in John Ainslie's forensic discussion of the nuclear dependency of Britain on the United States, and the implications of the decision to renew the Trident programme. Significant parts of the British military are deeply concerned about this decision, because it would pre-empt vast expenditures which would be likely to wipe out, for purely ideological reasons, spending on vital military equipment which they lack in their present wars. Officially, the nuclear weapons programme is supposed to cost between two and three per cent of the Defence Budget, or between seven hundred million pounds and one billion pounds every year. But the decision to renew the British deterrent entails enhancements to the specification of Trident which would undoubtedly constitute a breach of the Non-Proliferation Treaty, and the commissioning of new submarines which can carry them. So costly will this equipment prove that it has already put in jeopardy the programme of building the necessary new aircraft carriers to carry British forces into new wars for the greater glory of the American Empire. Perhaps we can manage without the aircraft carriers: but why on earth can we not also manage without the renewed deterrent?

Of course, renewed diplomatic goads and provocations might be souring relations with Russia to the point where various kinds of official unpleasantness are thinkable. There are days when it seems likely that the oligarchs have bought the Foreign Office as if it were a common or garden football club. But an all out nuclear war …? The need to be able to destroy what is left of Russia, after they have wiped out the British mainland? Where has prudence gone in these calculations?

Now the *Sunday Herald* has produced evidence which shows that all the planning presumptions upon which British weapons' designers have been working are in meltdown, because the American designers appear to have unilaterally set aside the formal exchange of letters between President Bush and Prime Minister Blair on the modalities of missile renewal. In December 2006, Prime Minister Blair wrote formally to President Bush:

> 'The United Kingdom wishes to ensure that any successor to the D5 system is compatible with, or is capable of being made compatible with, the launch system for the D5 missile, which we will in the meantime be installing in our new submarines ...'

Bush responded by inviting Britain to take part in the D5 replacement programme, or to discuss the extension of the planned life of the missiles.

> 'In this respect any successor to the D5 system should be compatible with, or be capable of being made compatible with, the launch system for the D5 missiles.'

But the *Sunday Herald* (22nd December 2007) presents evidence that American designers have asked for tenders for a test-bed for future underwater launched nuclear missiles, which implies the breakdown of the formal exchanges between Bush and Blair. The tenders specify a missile diameter of up to one hundred and twenty inches, while the diameter of Trident's outgoing D5 missile tubes is eighty-seven inches. The intention in preparing the new submarines was to begin by arming them with existing Trident missiles, only later replacing them with the new missiles currently being designed by the United States. The projected new American test-bed must not only be able to support missiles which are much larger than the present Trident ones, but also much heavier. The new missiles will be up to 200,000lbs, as opposed to the present missiles which weigh 130,000lbs.

The British military planners envisage maintaining the new submarines until at least 2055. But how the new submarines can be designed to cope with a missile whose dimensions remain fluid will be, as Ainslie was reported as saying in the *Herald*, 'a nightmare'.

Perhaps a bigger nightmare is the destruction of the Non-Proliferation Treaty, which all these new military decisions are calculated to accomplish. Was the NPT founded on illusions? Well, Gordon Brown is playing no small part in dissolving those illusions. What will we then have left but the continuous proliferation that we can already see in development?

Never was there a greater need for a rebirth of the peace movement, and a new campaign for nuclear disarmament.

Ken Coates

Is a nuclear-weapons-free world achievable?

Maj Britt Theorin

Dr. Theorin was a Member of both the Swedish and European Parliaments. She is a former Ambassador for Disarmament for her country, and gave this paper at a conference on the current dangers of nuclear weapons which was organised at the Parliament in Copenhagen by the Danish Pugwash Group in September 2007.

Where is the world heading – towards disaster, or towards reasonable solutions?

The violence a country uses can destroy its power, the author Hannan Arendt once said. The United States is moving rapidly along this road in Iraq and Iran. All empires disappear sooner or later – that is what we have learned from history – either through giving up power without using their capacity for violence, as the Soviets did under Gorbachev, or by letting violence destroy their power.

It seems that the leaders of the United States do not understand that the peoples of the world, who abolished the empires of the last centuries, are unwilling to be bound together for the supremacy of the US. The United States is at war in Iraq and Afghanistan, and seems to be planning an urgent attack on Iran, possibly with nuclear weapons.

In January 2007, prominent scientists moved forward the atomic Doomsday Clock, from seven minutes to five minutes before midnight. Midnight will be the end of civilisation. One of the reasons for this change was the increased threat of nuclear weapons.

The scientists warned of a second nuclear-weapons age. Serious threats include the 25,000 nuclear weapons in the United States and Russia, of which 2,000 are on high alert and can be discharged within minutes. Other serious threats include the ambitions of Iran and North Korea to go nuclear, increased terrorism, unsafe nuclear materials, for example, in Russia, and demands to increase civil nuclear power, which can increase the risk of spreading nuclear weapons.

In his Nuclear Posture Review of 2002, President Bush changed American nuclear-weapons doctrine in a very dangerous direction. He identified seven countries against which nuclear weapons can be *used*; five of those countries do not have nuclear weapons. Preventive attack, which in fact is forbidden in the UN Charter, was proposed in the new US nuclear weapons doctrine.

Risk of war in Iran

A recent study by Dan Plesch and Martin Butcher ('Considering a war with Iran', September 2007), using open sources, demonstrates that an attack on Iran can be massive and launched with surprise, rather than merely a contingency plan that needs months, if not years, of preparation. The study concludes that the United States has made military preparations to destroy Iran´s weapons of mass destruction, nuclear energy, regime, armed forces, state apparatus, and economic infrastructure within days, if not hours, of President Bush giving the order.

Any attack is likely to be on a massive scale on many fronts, but avoiding a ground invasion. Nuclear weapons are ready, but most unlikely to be used by the United States, the United Kingdom and Israel. The human, political and environmental effects would be devastating, while their military value is limited.

The United States is not publishing the scale of these preparations to deter Iran, tending to make confrontation more likely. The US retains the option of avoiding war, but using its forces as part of an overall strategy to shape Iran´s actions.

In the study the authors also point to eight arguments currently in circulation that deny the idea of a looming war.

How did we come to this current nuclear crisis?

For a couple of years, the nuclear energy ambitions of Iran have become an issue in world politics. What is true? Is Iran moving to become a nuclear-weapons power, or is Iran developing an exclusively peaceful nuclear energy industry? Iran has for some time been encouraged to cancel parts of its nuclear industry. This has been done by diplomatic pressure, which has lately been upgraded to gunboat diplomacy. The UN Security Council has enforced political sanctions against Iran. A military intervention has been discussed. These policies are unfortunate, unfair, and beside the point, says Jan Prawitz*, a Swedish scientist working on nuclear-weapons-free zones.

Today, Iran is criticized on three counts. One is that Iran has not complied with some of its reporting commitments to the International Atomic Energy Agency. Some reports were incomplete, delayed or just absent. Secondly, it was criticized for constructing an ultracentrifuge facility for enriching uranium. And, thirdly, it was criticized for constructing a nuclear reactor fuelled with natural uranium, and for producing a heavy water moderator for that reactor.

Primarily, it is the two latter projects that have attracted suspicion, because these facilities could be rearranged for production of weapons-grade uranium and plutonium. Even if Iran´s nuclear activities are today exclusively peaceful, once these facilities are fully completed, the lead time from a future decision to make nuclear weapons until fuel for a first explosive device will be available would be dramatically shortened.

According to 'worst-case-analysis', assuming that Iran has already decided to go nuclear, sufficient uranium for a first explosive device would be produced late

*On Iran and the current nuclear crisis in 'A Note on the Proposed Zone Free of Weapons of Mass Destruction in the Middle East', London, September 2007, Jan Prawitz, the Swedish Institute of International Affairs, Stockholm.

in the year 2010, if nothing goes wrong. To go from there to establish itself as a militarily significant nuclear power, would require an expensive and time consuming effort, says Prawitz.

The criticism for incomplete reporting by Iran is formally correct but still overemphasized. Incomplete reporting is not unusual among the Nuclear Non-Proliferation Treaty parties. Today, 31 of 185 non-nuclear states party have delayed concluding their reports by many years. Thus, while formally in error, Iran's behaviour is not extraordinarily dramatic.

It is more important for purposes of comparison that ultracentrifuge enrichment of uranium has gone on for several years in two non-nuclear-weapon states, Germany and Netherlands, and a new facility is being constructed in Brazil. Canada's whole nuclear power industry is based on natural uranium heavy water reactors. Some 50 tons of surplus plutonium is stockpiled in Japan. But these facts have caused no raised eyebrows in the UN Security Council.

Obviously, the current Iranian nuclear crisis is a substitute for other and wider political ambitions. Preventing the proliferation of weapons of mass destruction is a fundamentally important objective. But it is beside the point to approach that problem indirectly by requiring the limitation of fuel cycle elements on the part of non-nuclear-weapon states. The Security Council's demands are legally correct, but unfortunate. What Iran is doing is legally correct according to the Nuclear Non-Proliferation Treaty, which was agreed after careful negotiations and compromises during the years 1966 to 1968, says Jan Prawitz.

Are there no positive signs? Yes, there are – first, on Iran.

The Middle Powers Initiative pointed to the need for intensified diplomacy in a recent statement (20 September 2007). They say:

> 'Since 2003, Iran has met reporting requirements. In his report of 30 August 2007, International Atomic Energy Agency Director General ElBaradei stated that the Agency "is able to verify the non-diversion of declared nuclear material in Iran".
>
> The Agency and Iran have reached agreement on a work plan to clear up outstanding questions about Iran´s past nuclear activities. This plan must be given time to work.
>
> Iran has repeatedly indicated its openness to the operation of limited enrichment facilities in Iran under heightened Agency monitoring and with foreign participation.
>
> Finally, the United States and other nuclear weapon states can more credibly insist on Iranian compliance with its international obligations if they meet their own nuclear disarmament oligations ... The nuclear weapon states have, pursuant to their duties under the Nuclear Non-Proliferation Treaty, committed to a diminishing role for nuclear weapons in their security policies, and ... made commitments to the non-use of nuclear weapons against non-nuclear-weapon states that have signed the Treaty.'

Another interesting and positive sign appeared at the beginning of 2007. On 4 January, in the *Wall Street Journal* , there was an article by four architects of the Cold War – Republicans Henry Kissinger and George Schultz and Democrats William Perry and Sam Nunn – who demanded that the United States take a lead in the total abolition of *all* nuclear weapons. Their proposals where not new: in 1996, the Canberra Commission had proposed something similar, and, later on, so did the Blix Commission – taking nuclear weapons off alert; reducing the amount of nuclear weapons drastically; abolishing tactical nuclear weapons, and so on. I will come back to these proposals later. What is new is that these four politicians, who were formerly in favour of, and responsible for, nuclear weapons, now have an interest in common with the opponents of nuclear weapons and with civil society.

Arthur Schopenhauer, the philosopher, said that all truth passes through three stages; first, it is ridiculed; then, it is strongly counteracted; and, finally, it is suddenly accepted as obvious. Getting rid of all nuclear weapons has now, through these four politicians, reached the stage of being 'accepted as obvious'. The question is whether this truth has reached the American administration.

Why were these weapons developed?

More than 100 years ago, Dr Marie Curie discovered the radioactive elements radium and polonium. This was a big breakthrough in the medical area. Two decades later, it was possible to use the new discovery in heart diagnosis and other fatal diseases. In the beginning radioactivity saved lives. But, 47 years later, the same knowledge was used to produce the first nuclear weapons that destroyed Hiroshima and Nagasaki, killing then, and in the years to come, more than 200,000 people. This was a totally new way of warfare. The nuclear arms race that followed was unbelievable – the capacity could kill human beings not only once but several times over. Marie Curie's discovery turned out to be the biggest threat to world peace and security.

During the Second World War, the world feared that Hitler would develop atomic weapons. Nuclear scientists, among them Joseph Rotblat from Poland who lost his wife in a concentration camp, gave their knowledge to the Manhattan Project in order not to let the Nazis conquer the world. When they recognised that Hitler could not produce nuclear weapons, Joseph Rotblat proposed immediately that the project should stop, because there was no use any longer for such a horrible weapon. Politicians and the military rejected his proposal. When you could develop such an effective weapon, you could not stop it, even if the motive for it had disappeared. Rotblat lost his promised American citizenship and decided to devote his life to ridding the world of nuclear weapons. He became, in fact, the first opponent of nuclear weapons.

Nuclear weapons today

Today's stockpile of nuclear weapons has 700 times more explosive force than that used during the last century's big wars, which killed 44 million people. Today, there are thousands of nuclear weapons on missiles, submarines, ships and aircraft that are *on alert* all round the world. They are ready to be used within a minute. There exist today nuclear weapons so small that they can fit in a suitcase, beyond any treaty control.

Long after the end of the Cold War, around 30,000 nuclear weapons remain. Since 1945, more than 8 trillion dollars have been spent on nuclear weapons. In the shadow of the Cold War, the nuclear arms race increased.

The current destructive capacity of nuclear weapons is enormous. Any use would lead to catastrophe. The risk that nuclear weapons might be used by mistake or through miscalculation has increased. Political instability, unsafe control, and lack of proper management of nuclear weapons could lead to disaster.

On 25 January 1995, the world came close to the accidental use of nuclear weapons when the Russian military detected an unidentified ballistic missile over Norway, possibly heading for Russia. The order was given to Russian ballistic missile submarines to go to battle stations. Disaster was averted by only a few minutes when the missile was reassessed as harmless. Its identity and research mission had not reached the Russian early warning system. If such an incident were to occur when relations between the United States and Russia were not good, disaster might not be averted.

In April 1998, *The New England Journal of Medicine* published a special report which concluded that, despite the end if the Cold War, the risk of an accidental nuclear attack has increased. It pointed to the alarming number of US military personnel who had to be removed from involvement with nuclear weapons because of alcohol, drug abuse or psychiatric problems. The former four star General and Commander in Chief of US Strategic Air Command, Lee Butler, who had responsibility for all US Air Force and Navy nuclear deterrent forces and literally had had his finger on the button to release nuclear weapons, told the same story during the work in the Canberra Commission. He was absolutely convinced that the world needed to be free of all nuclear weapons.

What to do? Two examples

What has happened and what can be done to get rid of nuclear weapons? First of all, everyone has the responsibility and possibility to work to that end. I will give you two examples how one can work in order to move forward: the story of Joseph Rotblat, Pugwash and the Canberra Commission; and the story of getting nuclear weapons declared illegal.

Joseph Rotblat was one of the founders of the Pugwash Movement, which brought together scientists from East and West in order to build a bridge between the two opponents after the Second World War. After several years of work, Joseph was convinced that, in order to reach a world free of nuclear weapons, a plan had to be developed containing measures to reach this goal. All nuclear weapons must be forbidden and, step by step, destroyed, in the same way as other weapons of mass destruction such as chemical weapons and biological weapons.

And it *is* possible to abolish all nuclear weapons, technically, politically and economically – if the will exists. This was later confirmed in the report of the Canberra Commission, which was presented in 1996. The Prime Minister of Australia, Paul Keeting, was made aware of a book written by a group of scientists and others in the Pugwash movement – I was one of them – on the initiative of Joseph Rotblat.

The book was called *A nuclear-weapons-free-world – desirable, feasible?* Not everyone – nuclear scientists most of them – believed in Rotblat's goal that a nuclear-weapons-free world was feasible. Some of them saw Joseph as a dreamer. It was not possible to reach a nuclear-weapons-free world. The discussions were very hot and deep and Joseph argued well for his case – patient, dogged, but kindly. And, to the surprise of some of them, we managed to agree and the book was printed. It became the starting point.

The Canberra Commission

In December 1995, the Prime Minister of Australia, Paul Keeting, asked a group of experts to present a *realistic* plan of how *all* nuclear weapons could be abolished – not a dream but a realistic plan. We were sixteen men and one woman on the Commission. We had the best scientists providing us with excellent basic material, and many non-governmental organisations sent us their opinions. We had a full-time secretariat at our disposal. And we had nine months to prepare and deliver our Report.

The Commission members had different backgrounds and experiences: there were two four-star generals, Generals Lee Butler and Michael Carver; former US Secretary of Defence Robert McNamara; the former Prime Minister of France, Michel Rocard; several ambassadors and scientists and, of course, the 1995 Nobel Peace Price Winner, Joseph Rotblat.

We based the case for the elimination of nuclear weapons on three main arguments:

The first was that the destructiveness of nuclear weapons is so great that they *have no military utility* against a comparably equipped opponent, other than the belief that they deter that opponent from using nuclear weapons. Use of those weapons against a non-nuclear opponent *is politically and morally indefensible.*

The second argument was that the indefinite *deployment* of the weapons carries a high risk of their ultimate *use through accident or inadvertence.*

The last argument was that the possession of the weapons by some states *stimulates other nations to acquire them*, reducing security for all.

Immediate steps

We demanded that the nuclear weapons states at the highest political level should, once and for all, unanimously declare that they want to abandon all nuclear weapons, even if this is already stated in article 6 of the Nuclear Non-Proliferation Treaty, which they have all signed. Such a commitment would change instantly the tenor of the debate, the thrust of war planning, and the timing of, or indeed the necessity for, modernisation programmes.

This commitment must be accompanied by a series of practical, realistic and mutually reinforcing steps. As a start, without any negotiations, the nuclear weapons states can do several things which will immediately decrease the threat of nuclear weapons under which we all live. The first steps we proposed were:
● Taking nuclear weapons off alert
● Removal of warheads from delivery vehicles
● Ending deployment of non-strategic nuclear weapons

- Further reduction of United States and Russian nuclear arsenals
- Agreement among the nuclear weapon states of reciprocal no-first-use undertakings, and of a non-use undertaking by them in relation to the non-nuclear-weapon states.

To take nuclear weapons off alert will dramatically reduce the chance of an accidental or unauthorised launch of nuclear weapons. All nuclear weapons must be taken off alert. This could, in the first instance, be adopted by the nuclear weapons states unilaterally.

Separation of nuclear warheads from their delivery vehicles is a must, and they should be placed far from each other so that they cannot easily be put together again. The physical separation of warheads from vehicles would strongly reinforce the gains achieved by taking nuclear forces off alert.

The nuclear weapon states should unilaterally remove all non-strategic nuclear weapons from deployed sites to a limited number of secure storage facilities on *their own territory.*

A full stop for testing must be decided.

The nuclear weapon states should agree and state as soon as possible that they would not be the first to use or threaten to use nuclear weapons against each other, and that they would not use or threaten to use nuclear weapons in any conflict with a non-nuclear-weapon state. This would lead to an important and total change in the nuclear weapons strategy of the nuclear weapons states. All this can be done without delaying negotiations.

Reinforcing steps

Many other proposals are to be found in the report:
- Action to prevent further horizontal proliferation
- Developing verification arrangements for a nuclear-weapon-free world with an international ban on research, storing, selling and the use of nuclear weapons
- Cessation of the production of fissile material for nuclear explosive purposes.

Effective verification is critical to the achievement and maintenance of a nuclear-weapon-free world. Concurrent with the central disarmament process, there will be a need for activity to build an environment conducive to nuclear disarmament and non-proliferation. The spread of nuclear-weapon-free zones world-wide could progressively codify the transition to a world free of nuclear weapons.

The Canberra Commission Report was not a dream but a *realistic* way of eliminating all nuclear weapons. Joseph Rotblat had really come close to his faith. The issue had left the academic world and turned onto the political level.

Even if the Canberra Commission Report did not directly have a result, the Non-Proliferation Treaty conference of 2000 included in its thirteen practical steps the proposals of the Canberra Commission (see box). The Non-Proliferation Treaty is the most important international treaty on nuclear weapons, in which nuclear weapon states commit themselves to getting rid of nuclear weapons, and non-nuclear-weapon states commit themselves not to seek nuclear weapons. Every fifth year the Treaty is up for review.

Summery of the thirteen practical steps for nuclear disarmament agreed at the NPT Review Conference in 2000

1. Early entry into force of the Comprehensive Nuclear Test-Ban Treaty (CTBT)

2. A moratorium on nuclear tests pending the CTBT's entry into force.

3. Conclude negotiations in the Conference on Disarmament on a verifiable fissile materials treaty within five years.

4. Establish a subsidiary body in the Conference on Disarmament to deal with nuclear disarmament.

5. Apply the principle of irreversibility to nuclear disarmament and arms control.

6. An unequivocal undertaking by the nuclear-weapon states to eliminate their nuclear arsenals.

7. Entry into force of the Strategic Arms Reduction Treaty (START II); conclusion of START III; preserve and strengthen the Anti-Ballistic Missile Treaty.

8. Completion and implementation of the Trilateral Initiative between the United States, Russia and the International Atomic Energy Agency.

9. Steps by the nuclear-weapon states leading to nuclear disarmament in a way that promotes international stability, based on the principle of undiminished security for all:
● unilateral reductions;
● increased transparency;
● the further reduction of non-strategic nuclear weapons;
● de-alerting;
● A diminishing role for nuclear weapons in security policies;
● The engagement by all the nuclear-weapon states in disarmament as soon as appropriate

10. Arrangements by nuclear-weapon states to place fissile material no longer required for military purposes under IAEA supervision or other relevant international verification.

11. Reaffirmation that the ultimate objective is general and complete disarmament under effective international control.

12. Regular reports within the NPT: strengthened review process.

13. Improved verification of compliance with nuclear disarmament agreements.

The Non-Proliferation Treaty 2000 is signed by all Member States, including the nuclear weapon states, which committed themselves to this action programme to rid the world of nuclear weapons and is still valid. All signatories to the NPT should be made aware of their duty to fulfil what they promised. We have to remind them.

The Canberra Commission Report, the Non-Proliferation Treaty 2000, and the report entitled 'Weapons of Terror' (with the subtitle 'Freeing the World of Nuclear, Biological and Chemical Arms' – the Blix Report of 2006) reflect Joseph Rotblat's ideas and proposals of ways towards a world free of nuclear weapons. All of them are still valid and represent sound and realistic ways of ridding the world of all nuclear weapons.

Illegality

In July 1996, at the end of our work in the Canberra Commission, the International Court of Justice in The Hague gave its response to a request from the General Assembly of the United Nations for an advisory opinion on the legality of the threat or use of nuclear weapons.

For a long time, the International Association of Lawyers Against Nuclear Arms (IALANA) had tried to get the question of illegality of nuclear weapons on the agenda. In the 1980s, my own civil servants in the Swedish Foreign Ministry told me when I was an ambassador responsible for our disarmament policy that it would be impossible to obtain a response that made nuclear weapons illegal.

The international lawyers decided to try to bring the question to the General Assembly of the United Nations, and formulated a resolution requesting an advisory opinion from the International Court. It was taken on board by some states. A full-scale war almost broke out in the UN. I was there and could see with my own eyes how the United States went into the room of the non-aligned states and put pressure on many small countries that relied on the US for economic or other support. Such a resolution was unacceptable for US.

The first year, the resolution was not put forward. But the next year the resolution was brought to the General Assembly, even though the United States had, in the meantime, used all its power to threaten many small countries. And to the surprise of many, the resolution was adopted by the General Assembly with a clear majority. Sweden, which then had a Conservative government, abstained from voting. Now began the next step for those of us who wanted to see a positive answer. We had to influence the International Court and our own governments.

When the International Court received the request, it turned to its member states and asked for their opinion before the Court could give an answer. As my government had lost the election, I had to do the work in the Parliament. I put forward a resolution, signed by all political parties except the Conservatives, demanding that the Swedish government respond to the Court that the position of Sweden was that the use or threat to use nuclear weapons was illegal. Of course, the Parliament adopted the resolution, and in the very last minutes, with the help of some political pressure, we managed to get the government to respond that 'the Parliament – not the government – has the opinion that the use of nuclear weapons is illegal'.

This work in Sweden, and the efforts of many other people in lobbying their own governments, achieved a result. In July 1996, the Court declared that the use or threat of using nuclear weapons was not in accordance with international law. This was a very important victory for public opinion!

The declared illegality of nuclear weapons is a result of pressure from public opinion, experts and scientists, and the involvement of engaged politicians. It is a good example of how we can work in the future.

There are many more examples of the pressures exerted by ordinary people which have changed nuclear policy – stopping the deployment of medium-range nuclear weapons in different European countries; stopping the development of the neutron bomb, which leaves houses and property standing but kills human beings; stopping nuclear testing by France through a boycott of French wines, just to mention a few examples. In Sweden our boycott of French wines led to a 50 per cent decrease in sales, and even involved restaurant owners who threw bottles of champagne into the street in front of the television cameras.

*   *   *

Where is the world heading? Towards disaster, or towards reasonable solutions? Towards war in Iran, or towards diplomatic solutions? Towards a new nuclear arms race, or towards nuclear disarmament? Towards mass murder with nuclear weapons, or towards the UN Charter's provision that peace shall be created by peaceful means? It depends on us – if we are willing to take responsibility and act with persistence and conviction. Everyone can do something. International law, the facts, and realistic programmes are already there – the UN Charter, the Canberra Commission Report, the Blix Commission Report, and the Nuclear Non-Proliferation Treaty action programme in 13 steps.

With facts and determination we can change the world. I am convinced that, one day, Joseph Rotblat's dream and our dream – a nuclear-weapon-free world – will come true.

Nuclear disarmament – still waiting

Mayors for Peace

The United States maintains hundreds of nuclear weapons outside its own territory, many at bases in Europe. It conducts regular exercises with these weapons. Mayors for Peace, the international organisation led by the Mayor of Hiroshima, Dr. Tadatoshi Akiba, recently published this appeal against their deployment.

On 8 December 2007, we marked the twentieth anniversary of the historic Intermediate-Range Nuclear Forces (INF) Treaty. The Treaty, an agreement between the United States and the Soviet Union, was signed in Washington DC on 8 December 1987 by President Ronald Reagan and General Secretary Mikhail Gorbachev. The treaty eliminated nuclear and conventional ground-launched ballistic and cruise missiles with ranges of 500 to 5,500 kilometres (300 to 3,400 miles). By the Treaty's 1 June 1991 deadline, a total of 2,692 such weapons had been destroyed, 846 by the United States and 1,846 by the Soviet Union.

The Treaty was concluded after years of high tension between the United States and the Soviet Union. It put an end to the deployment of mid-range nuclear weapons in five Nato member states: Belgium (at Florennes), Germany (at Mutlangen), Italy (at Comiso), The Netherlands (at Woensdrecht), and the United Kingdom (at Greenham Common and Molesworth).

These deployments had inspired, in the streets of western capitals, some of the largest demonstrations in human history, as the spectre of nuclear annihilation loomed over humanity. The Intermediate-Range Nuclear Forces Treaty marked the start of an era of détente between the Soviet Union and the West. In December 1989, Gorbachev and George H.W. Bush declared the Cold War officially over, at a summit in Malta.

During the Cold War, Europe was divided between the transatlantic military alliances of Nato and the Warsaw Pact, made up of the Soviet Union, Bulgaria, Czechoslovakia, East Germany, Hungary, Poland and Romania. The Warsaw Pact was officially dissolved on 1 July 1991, soon after the end of the Cold War. The Soviet Union withdrew its nuclear weapons from Ukraine and Belarus, now independent states.

Unfortunately, Nato didn't follow Russia's actions, and US tactical nuclear weapons remained in Belgium, Germany, Greece, Italy, the Netherlands, Turkey, and the UK. Today, the United States is the only nuclear weapon state to deploy its nuclear weapons on the territories of non-nuclear weapon states. This, for many, violates the spirit of Articles I and II of the Nuclear Non-Proliferation Treaty (NPT).

Many of these nuclear weapon deployments have become militarily obsolete. Because of their short range, they can only reach targets within new European Union member states. Indeed, wherever based or targeted, their use would not be politically viable. It would appear that the main purpose of these deployments is political not military, i.e. to signal allegiance to the use of nuclear force, *per se*.

These deployments continue to be characterised by a high level of secrecy and lack of transparency. Questions by members of national parliaments in the countries where the weapons are deployed are always met with a 'neither confirm nor deny' response, reflecting official Nato policy. This makes it very difficult, if not impossible, to have an honest democratic debate.

A Greenpeace International survey, in 2006, showed that the public in the six concerned countries are not aware of the deployment of nuclear weapons on their territories. Yet they are regularly provided alarming media reports of nuclear dangers in Iraq, North Korea or Iran. We all know today that the current war in Iraq was started over non-existent weapons of mass destruction. What is supposed to be a well-informed Western audience is living in ignorance of thousands of potential Hiroshimas stored in their own backyards. The same survey showed that, once informed about the presence of US nuclear weapons on their territory, a large majority of the public wants them to be withdrawn.

On 8 July 1996, the International Court of Justice (ICJ) in The Hague ruled: 'There exists an obligation to pursue in good faith and bring to a conclusion negotiations leading to nuclear disarmament in all its aspects.' Here the Court was clearly referring to Article VI of the Nuclear Non-Proliferation Treaty. The Treaty, signed by 188 states, does not deal only with the proliferation of nuclear weapons to non-nuclear weapon states such as Iran. When signed in 1968, the Treaty also imposed an obligation on the nuclear weapon states to move swiftly and in good faith towards complete nuclear disarmament.

The unwillingness of the nuclear weapon states to negotiate a global treaty banning all nuclear weapons has been frustrating for most governments. For decades, the United Nations General Assembly has been adopting nuclear disarmament resolutions, with large majorities. The United States, Israel, France and the United Kingdom have been champions in resisting substantial progress towards complete nuclear disarmament. In 2006, the United States announced plans to produce new so-called 'Reliable Replacement Warheads'. In 2007, the UK announced the replacement of its nuclear Trident system, while France is testing a new nuclear M-51 missile.

During one of his last speeches as UN Secretary General, on 22 November 2006, Kofi Annan said: 'While governments are coming together to address many global threats, the one area where there is a total lack of any common strategy is the one that may well present the greatest danger of all — the area of nuclear weapons'. Annan added, during a lecture at Princeton University: 'We are asleep at the controls of a fast-moving aircraft ... An aircraft, of course, can remain airborne only if both wings are in working order. We cannot choose between non-proliferation and disarmament. We must tackle both tasks with the urgency they demand.'

Even during the height of the Cold War there were already calls for a nuclear-weapon-free world. On 15 January 1986, Gorbachev announced a Soviet proposal for a ban on all nuclear weapons by 2000, including intermediate-range nuclear force missiles in Europe. This was dismissed by the United States.

Twenty years later, however, on 4 January 2007, Henry Kissinger, Sam Nunn, William Perry and George Schultz made a remarkable call for complete nuclear disarmament in the *Wall Street Journal*. Warning that in the post-Cold War world, reliance on nuclear weapons is becoming 'increasingly hazardous', they asked: 'can the promise of the Nuclear Non-Proliferation Treaty and the possibilities envisioned at Reykjavik be brought to fruition?' We believe that a major effort should be launched by the United States to produce a positive answer through concrete stages.'

On the twentieth anniversary of the Intermediate-Range Nuclear Forces Treaty, our task is to develop practical steps to advance the 2020 Vision campaign launched by Mayor Tadatoshi Akiba of Hiroshima, and now supported by over 1800 mayors worldwide, to rid the world of nuclear weapons by the year 2020.

Nato members Belgium, Germany, Italy, the Netherlands, Turkey and the United Kingdom have, to date, accepted deployment of US nuclear weapons on their territories. But, membership of NATO does not require any state to accept nuclear deployments. For example, Greece stopped hosting US nuclear weapons in 2001. Let us take control of this fast-moving aircraft and, as an important step, remove the last foreign deployed nuclear weapons from the territory of another state. That would also be a step towards a new Nato defence policy not reliant on nuclear weapons.

Submitted by the Executive Committee of Mayors for Peace, representing network of 1,937 mayors in 126 countries

> Dr. Tadatoshi Akiba, Mayor of Hiroshima, Japan
> Mr. Tomihisa Taue, Mayor of Nagasaki, Japan
> Mr. Donald L. Plusquellic, Mayor of Akron, Ohio, USA; past President, U.S. Conference of Mayors
> Mr. Leonardo Domenici, Mayor of Firenze, Italy
> Mr. Bernd Strauch, Deputy Mayor of Hannover, Germany
> Mr. Patrik Vankrunkelsven, Senator; former Mayor of Laakdal, Belgium
> Ms. Catherine Margate, Mayor of Malakoff, France
> Mr. Glynn Evans, Deputy Mayor of Manchester, UK
> Mr. Luc Deheane, Mayor of Ypres, Belgium

and Mayors of cities near to European military bases where US nuclear weapons are deployed:

> Mr. Stefano Del Cont, Mayor of Aviano, Italy

Ms. Anna Giulia Guarneri, Mayor of Ghedi, Italy
Mr. Theo Kelchtermans, Mayor of Peer, Belgium
Ms. Dr. Joke W. Kersten, Mayor of Uden, The Netherlands
Mr. Heinz Onnertz, District Administrator, Kreis Vulkaneiffel, Germany
Mr. Vedat Karadag, Mayor of Incirlik, Turkey

More information about Mayors for Peace is available online (www.2020visioncampaign.org).

COMMUNICATION
WORKERS UNION

No Trident
replacement

Billy Hayes
General Secretary

Jane Loftus
President

The cost of nukes

Jacqueline Cabasso

Jackie Cabasso is Executive Director of the Western States Legal Foundation (www.wslfweb.org) in the United States.

It was recently reported that funding for the so-called 'reliable replacement warhead' (RRW) had been zeroed out in the fiscal year 2008 budget passed by the United States Congress. This may be an important symbolic 'victory' – time will tell, especially following the rejection of the robust nuclear earth penetrator. It seems to signal that Congress is uncomfortable with the idea of funding new nuclear weapons. Nonetheless, it is a very small thing.

Over the years since the end of the Cold War, nuclear weapon types specifically named in budget line items have been zeroed out several times, reappearing under different names or buried in more vaguely identified budget categories. Remember, also, that there is an officially acknowledged 'black budget' about which we know nothing. And, bear in mind that even with a few million cut from the reliable replacement warhead, the overall nuclear weapons research and development budget is enormous, and still higher than during the average Cold War years. Most importantly, zeroing out the reliable replacement warhead this year doesn't fundamentally change anything about US nuclear weapons policy, posture, readiness, capability, threat or lethality. Here are a few examples.

First, the Stockpile Life Extension Program is going forward. The last time I checked, the Labs were working on the W-76 warhead, giving it an enhanced ground burst capability, which would improve its first strike capability. 'Life extensions' are planned for other warhead models. This begs the question of what 'new' means, when talking about a nuclear warhead.

Second, despite the claim made by the US representative to the First Committee of the United Nations in October 2007, that US nuclear weapons are not now and have never been on 'hair trigger' alert, they do, in fact, remain on high alert status, and have taken on an even more central role in US 'Global Strike' planning, which has as much or more to do with the delivery systems than the warheads. According to Bruce Blair's rebuttal: 'Both the United States and Russia today maintain about one-third of their total strategic arsenals on launch-ready alert. Hundreds of missiles armed with thousands of nuclear warheads the equivalent of about 100,000 Hiroshima bombs – can be launched within a very few minutes. *The end of the Cold War did not lead the United States and Russia to significantly change their nuclear strategies or the way they operate their nuclear forces.*'

Third, the United States is the only nuclear weapon state that deploys nuclear weapons on foreign territory. It is reliably estimated that 350 US B-61 nuclear bombs are deployed at the following Nato bases in Europe: Aviano, Italy (50); Ghedi, Italy (40); Peer, Belgium (20); Uden, The Netherlands (20); Vulkaneiffel, Germany (20); Incirlik, Turkey (90); Lakenheath, UK (110).

Fourth, in response to the article signed by European mayors who want the US nukes removed from their territories, the Nato Chief announced that there are no plans to change Nato's nuclear policy.

Fifth, almost nobody talks about the delivery systems or the long planning horizons always in place for nuclear weapons systems. Consider the following: 'Advisers to US Strategic Command this month urged the Defense Department to begin research and development soon for a new nuclear-weapons submarine, according to the Navy ... The Review anticipated that a new program would have to begin around 2016 for the first submarine to be fielded in 2002. However, defense sources have told *Global Security Newswire* that it now appears initial funding would be sought by 2010.' Note the reliance on the 2002 Nuclear Posture Review, widely dismissed by the arms control community at the time as a mere 'wish list.')

Sixth, the details are in the fine print. With everyone continuing to sing the praises of Kissinger, Shultz, Perry and Nunn for their call for a 'nuclear weapon free world', Kissinger and Shultz have endorsed Sidney Drell's position that 'research work on new reliable replacement warhead designs should certainly go ahead'. The history of military research and development strongly suggests that such efforts are not necessarily limited to specific weapon designs, and that even if a particular design in terminated, research and development may very well lead to new weapons concepts or modifications. It's not over till its over.

Seventh, the draft environmental impact statement for the nuclear weapons 'Complex Transformation' (formerly Complex 2030) is expected. I predict with a high degree of confidence that it will not include a plan for closing down the nuclear weapons infrastructure because the reliable replacement warhead isn't currently funded. So what are they planning to spend that $150 billion on over the next 25 years?

Eighth, The reliable replacement warhead vote not withstanding, the United States is not in any way, shape or form acting in good faith with regard to its Nuclear Non-Proliferation Treaty Article VI obligation to negotiate 'in good faith' the end of the arms race 'at an early date' and 'nuclear disarmament in all its aspects'.

Finally, the *Encarta Encyclopaedia* describes militarism as 'advocacy of an ever-stronger military as a primary goal of society, even at the cost of other social priorities and liberties'. It relates militarism to chauvinism, fascism, and national socialism. As uncomfortable as it may be for many, this chilling definition accurately describes the historical trajectory and current reality of US national security policy. The threatened first use of nuclear weapons remains at the heart of that policy. While it's important to celebrate small 'victories', we need to keep our eyes on the prize.

It is not at all certain that removal of funding for the reliable replacement warhead is the result of efforts by anti-nuclear activists. There are a couple of Congress members, Hobson and Visclosky, who didn't like the reliable replacement warhead from the beginning, for reasons of their own. I believe it would be intellectually dishonest to proclaim this a major victory. After I wrote my initial response, I read the summary and explanatory statement that accompany the joint House-Senate omnibus appropriations bill, the fiscal year 2008 Consolidated Appropriations Act. I found no surprises. According to the official summary, the nuclear weapons budget is the same as fiscal year 2007, and the reliable replacement warhead isn't even gone, it's just on hold:

> 'Weapons Programs: $6.3 billion, the same as 2007 and $214 million below the President's request.
>
> Reliable Replacement Warhead: Prohibits the development of a reliable replacement warhead until the President develops a strategic nuclear weapons plan to guide transformation and downsizing of the stockpile and nuclear weapons complex.'

The explanatory statement provides a detailed breakdown of the funded nuclear weapons activities, including further description of the reliable replacement warhead and a new science campaign called 'Advanced Certification', and goes on to talk about the Stockpile Life Extension Program. Under 'Warhead Dismantlement' you will find funding for the Device Assembly Facility at the Nevada Test Site, for 'additional missions'. Read on to discover funding for the 'enhanced test readiness program', Inertial Confinement Fusion including the National Ignition Facility at the Livermore Lab and the Z machine at Sandia, Advanced Simulation and Computing, including academic partnerships, and pit manufacturing and certification. And it goes on.

To sum up, one small line item was cut, the fiscal year 2007 funding level was maintained, and the deck chairs were rearranged on the *Titanic*.

I believe that it is imperative to broaden our approach, and to educate ourselves and the public about the profound historical and economic underpinnings of the military-industrial-academic complex. Imagine a scenario in which tens or hundreds of thousands of people around the country were calling unambiguously for the abolition of nuclear weapons and war and demanding meaningful leadership from the United States. What kind of political space might be opened up, and what kind of results might one expect? Certainly, not less than eliminating three letters (reliable replacement warhead) from the National Nuclear Security

Administration's vocabulary. We might actually get more and, in the process, begin to generate a real national debate on the purpose of, and therefore the future of, nuclear weapons, and the requirements for genuine human and ecological security.

Conversion Currency

Alexis Lykiard
[23.12.2007]

Add extra glad tidings to Christmas Two Owe Owe Seven:
EX-PM BLAIR IN SECT-CHANGE! FAST-TRACK I.D. TO HEAVEN!
Popes buy the best lies – what price the warmonger's Amen?
Are men who 'honestly believe' so smoothly 'born again'?
Doubtless the balm of confession soon expiates all guilt,
And holy oil shall sanctify whatever blood is split.

Willie and Maud

An original screenplay by

Trevor Griffiths

Trevor Griffith's two volumes of Theatre Plays *are published by Spokesman, together with his celebrated screenplays of the life of Thomas Paine,* These Are the Times, *and of D. H. Lawrence's* Sons and Lovers. *A new volume of screenplays, including 'Willie and Maud', is forthcoming.*

black

MAUD'S VOICE: *My dear Willie, What on earth is going on? I hear from my publisher in London you have had my manuscript for months and will neither give your consent to its publication nor furnish him with reasons why you object. Can this be true? I know things have been cool between us for a long time now and I have been perhaps too ready to lambast you in public for your increasingly appalling politics …*

fade up

title*: red on black: 'Willie and Maud'*

MAUD'S VOICE: (Continues) *… but I have never ever thought of you as other than a dear and true friend. Am I mistaken? Please tell me how we might resolve this matter. To you it may seem a literary event of little moment, but it is my story and I wish to see it published and I hate the thought you may be playing games with it out of some whim or other.*

black

fade up

caption*: none of this happened …*

black

MAUD'S VOICE: *I must have answer soon. Tell me you will help. Always your friend, Maud.*

caption*: Dublin Bay, summer, 1938*

becoming

a long white room *salmoned by dipping sun; plaster walls hung with occult symbols and scrolled texts, a stand of tibetan windbells, a burmese gong, african masks, open windows catching sea sound, a simple desk and chair, a divan bed, persian rugs on plain wood floor. A man's voice intones a not quite intelligible mantra over and over. We reach*

Willie*, tranced, crosslegged on a rug, a single red rose in his hands, face to the sun, at 71 his own Prospero, the mantra pulsing up from him like throatsong: my maudmy maudmy maud my maud my maud …*

the room again; photographs, portraits, sketches, letters, candles, incense burners and hands of cards dealt from the tarot encircle the squatting **Willie** and pen him to the wall at his back.

his face, eyes in shadow, most else below blooded and bruised by a sinking sun. The mantra breaks to silence. The eyes blink open, probe deep into the thickening light.

the windows, afire with light, the mantra resumed, stronger, more insistent. Something begins to form in the windowed effulgence, not quite shape and not yet colour; an immanence.

a large rear garden terrace, evening, alive with kids at play and grown-ups at ease around the place; and several monkeys, a huge irish wolfhound, rabbits, a donkey, a goat and a wilderness of cats being themselves everywhere. We reach

Maud, 70 or so, tall and beautiful still, at a trestle table a touch apart from her family, an inveterate smoker's cigarette in her lips, revising a typed manuscript, voicing phrases as she goes. Across the table, her 4 year old grandson **Tiernan** crayons a bold black and red picture of her. She looks up suddenly, hearing something somewhere.

the room again; **Willie's** face, peering, beginning to see, his hand stretching towards the light, opening slowly, offering up the dark red rose it holds;

the windows, the vague figure forming of a tall iconically attractive **Maud** in her Cathleen Ní Houlihan incarnation forty years back.

garden again, Maud scanning the trees for the source of the sound, a strange soughing mymaudmymaud.

TIERNAN: *(from nowhere)* Willie!

She frowns at the still crayoning boy across the table.

MAUD: What did you say?

The lad looks up, face blank, unaware he spoke. His mother **Kit** *leaves the house for the terrace, an envelope held aloft in her hand.*

KIT: For you, Maud. And by hand, by God.

room again, **Willie's** *face, a slow smile of achievement in the darkening silence. The door creaks open,* **George Hyde-Lees**, *his wife, mid-forties, stands in the doorway at the head of the stairs, dressed for off.*

GEORGE: Willie my car's here I shall need to leave if I'm to catch my boat …
    (His head turns slowly to take her in) I've left lists everywhere, Mr Sweeney has agreed to do for you while I'm away.

WILLIE: … Mr Sweeney ..? Where are you going?

GEORGE: *(patient, measured)* … Willie, I'm going to visit my parents, in London, not my idea, darling, yours … You dreamt they were in danger ..? *(He's creaking to his feet)* You promised me you wouldn't use the lotus position any more.

WILLIE: Leave me if you must, but do not I beg you leave me with that … *(Car-horn from below)* … Sweeney …

He waves a hand for emphasis, she sees the rose in it.

GEORGE: *(Casual, threading gloves on)* … Who is it he's to collect at the station tomorrow by the way? Come.

She holds out a cheek for his lips, he approaches with care, kisses her cheek, then her neck.

GEORGE: There's nothing in the diary.

WILLIE: It'll be some student, I imagine. Slipped my mind. *(Nuzzles her neck)* I hate you being away.

GEORGE: *(soft)* Will I stay?

WILLIE: *(eventually)* No no, off you go. I'm just a foolish fond old man. But hurry back.

GEORGE: Take your pills. Promise?

He nods. She blows him a kiss from the door. Closes it behind her. He dwells for a time, resummoning the moment. Crosses to his desk. Lays the rose on it, across a photograph of Maud at 17 at St Patrick's Hall in her coming-out gown. Her father Tommy in dress uniform, the Prince of Wales and his son Clarence, make up the formal shot.

garden*; **Maud** stands by a clump of trees reading the note.*

WILLIE'S VOICE: (Over) *My Dear Maud, Your letter caught up with me here at the Summer House en route for France. Pack a weekend bag and take the four o'clock to Howth Station on Friday, a car will be there to meet you, it's the only way if we're to resolve this matter of your book before I'm gone…*

The child calls her to look, the finished picture held up in his hands: the tall stick-figure grandmother in black stands half as tall again as her red house.

Howth Station*, platform; a straggle of holidaymakers leaving the fuming train. The figure of **Maud** appears apparitionally through the clearing steam; tall, erect, in black habit and veil, her bags at her feet.*

WILLIE'S VOICE: (Continuing over) *… I have wanted to see you for a long time now but … I am still Yours Ever, Willie.*

A short odd donkey of a man, boots and waistcoat, clatters up to meet her.

SWEENEY: *(Heavy Sligo)* Sweeney himself, sent to serve the Royal Queen of Eireann, this way if ye will, Your Holiness.

He gathers her bags, leads her off to the ticket-barrier, calling for those ahead to give way. Word ripples around the place, folk begin to surround her, keen to press the famous flesh.

upper windows *overlooking the sea road, a gleaming, spruced-up **Willie** watching and waiting. A battered '28 Model A sways and chatters round the bend of the hill, **Willie** edges back into shadow, eyes bright in the dark of the room.*

car*, rattling up to the headland, the sea a dark glisten beyond. The house ahead begins to loom. **Maud** hangs on grimly.*

SWEENEY: *(Crazy at the wheel)* So will ye stay the whole weekend, Your Grace? My wife'll be cookin', she'll need to know, we do for the Great Man when the lady's away.

MAUD: *(Bumped and banged)* George is away? He made no mention.

SWEENEY: Packed off to London like a piece of luggage last Wednesday, didn't I take her meself for the train. Yer Man's a pot cat stuffed with secrets, so he is. *(Swinging the wheel)* Hold tight to your teeth there, milady!

High shot of the car screeching from the road into the grounds of the headland house and clattering eventually to a stop by a rear door.

*Half-heard, at distance, as **Sweeney** helps her out and shepherds her inside:*

SWEENEY: And here y'are, safe and sound, Your Worship. I'll set ye in the library and let yer Man know you're come … Mind your step there.

*The shot angles upwards, locates **Willie** at his window, watching everything. Voices fade, a door's pulled to down below. The figure at the window fades back in to the room. Silence.*

A Burmese gong begins to hum, slow, low, resonant.

Titles *end.*

Fade to black.

INT. DAY. THE YEATS' SUMMER HOUSE; BOOK-LINED FRONT ROOM.

A Siamese cat in gleaming black ceramic stares out from the mantelpiece in the half-bright room. The gong hums on, somewhere above.

Maud stands at the mantel, cloak discarded, gazing at the pot cat. Sounds of a rumbling spat drift in from the back of the house: Willie does not require the Sweeneys to sleep in while George is away; Sweeney will not hear of it.

She turns away from the mantel, reads the familiar room, touches known objects, is in turn touched by them; studies pictures and photographs of Willie through the years, one of herself as Cathleen; takes in framed scrolls on the walls announcing his Nobel Prize or the Freedom of some city. The spat grumbles on.

She reaches the desk, stops to light a cigarette, sees her manuscript on the leather writing pad, turns it carefully round with her fingers, begins to leaf pages, checks for marginal notes, finds none. Frowns. Leafs on a little.

Sudden laughter down the garden. Voices, a man's, a woman's, deep in talk, drift in. She returns the MS to the desk, crosses to the window, scans the long lawn and orchard, fence, cliff and sea beyond. A pair of lovers out for the day drift into frame, out at the cliff's edge. The pale young man wants something of her, the auburn-haired young woman won't give it. Maud stares intently, drawn as if to a scene from her own life.

WILLIE looms up behind her at the window. For a moment both are gazing out in silence.

WILLIE: *(Soft)* Ghosts, is it?

MAUD: *(A smile)* Shouldn't wonder. Hello Willie.

She turns to look at him.

WILLIE: Look at you.

He moves in to kiss her cheek.

WILLIE: How long is it ..? Ten years?

MAUD: Must be.

WILLIE: An age. An ice age. And my God, look at you.

He steps back to admire her. She takes a look at the tanned, still handsome man. Chuckles.

WILLIE: What?

MAUD: Nothing.

WILLIE: *(Checking his front)* What is it?

MAUD: It's nothing. Really. Your pullover, it's back to front.

WILLIE: *(Trying to check)* Is it? How do you know?

MAUD: I can see it is … *(He begins removing it)* Willie, please, it doesn't matter, leave it …

WILLIE: See, no label, how does one tell?

MAUD: The front's supposed to sit lower than the back. See …

WILLIE: *(A sniff)* I see what I see.

MAUD: Said a blind man to a star.

WILLIE: Who used to say that? Was it George Russell?

MAUD: Or was it Oscar? I can't remember.

They share a chuckle.

WILLIE: It's not easy being A Great Poet, you know. Have you any idea how much respect and awe I command in people these days …? They're so busy bowing and scraping they don't have chance to notice my damned jumper's on back to front.

MAUD: I bet you love that. More deference, I'll try to remember …

She puts her cigarette case back in her bag, lays it on a table. His eyes never leave her.

Outside, the Young Man's raised voice, angry, fearful, calling his lover not to go: Cathleen, Cathleen.

MAUD: Your man tells me George is away.

WILLIE: London. Family. She was sad to miss you. He's not my man, by the way, he does odd jobs about the place. But it leaves the decks clear. The boat ready to sail. And all the time we need for the dark uncharted waters up ahead …

She shivers a little, sensing undisclosed agendas, games perhaps. Lights another cigarette.

MAUD: It's only a little book, Willie. I was rather hoping for plain sailing.

He gives no answer. Swings suddenly to look at the doorway. Sweeney's there already, as if cued or magically summoned.

WILLIE: *(Glacial)* Sweeney.

SWEENEY: Himself, sirrah.

WILLIE: Kindly show Madame to her room.

SWEENEY: That I will, your honour.

WILLIE: And see she has what she needs. If I'm wanted for anything, I'll be in my lair. *(Turns away, finished with him)* Rest. We'll talk it through at dinner.

He smiles, turns to leave. Sweeney hasn't budged.

WILLIE: What is it?

SWEENEY: Sligo Hare.

WILLIE: Sligo Hare?

SWEENEY: Y'asked to know what the wee woman's makin' yez for dinner, it's Sligo Hare.

WILLIE: Sligo Hare. What is it?

SWEENEY: Chicken.

Silence. Willie's eyes burn into the little man.

MAUD: *(Finally)* Just take my bags if ye would, Mr Sweeney, I'll find my own way up.

He evaporates. Willie's on the edge, trying not to blow.

MAUD: Strange man. Is he always so ..?

WILLIE: *(Blowing)* … This man is sent to dog my days and nip me to the grave, Maud. We have built a new Ireland, with a theatre and a literature and painting second to very few, and we have peopled it with … Sweeneys, with oafs and dullards, common beasts without a scrap of culture or a thought higher than the muck they stand in, you know the Irish for Sweeney, Maud ..? *Suibhne*, peasant, same root as swine …

He searches a chair, sits heavily, riven with the pain of it. Sweat beads his head and hair. He dabs it with a kerchief. She hangs on, concerned, a bit disturbed by the venom.

MAUD: Can I get you something?

WILLIE: Forgive me, it … I … he, that man, that …

MAUD: Stop it, Willie, you hurt yourself *(She takes out a handkerchief, stoops to wipe his head and hair)* Now relax. And breathe. And breathe. And breathe.

WILLIE: *(Coming back)* Bless you. *(He stills the hand she dries him with, gently kisses it.)* Oh. I have missed you so much. For so much of my life. Missed. Lacked. Wanted. And for a moment: here you are. Woman of the Sidhe. Queen Maeve. Cathleen Ní Houlihan. Madame Republic. *(He leans his head back.)* I'm better. Go.

MAUD: You missed one. Maud Gonne Mad they call me now. *(She smiles, squeezes his hand, kisses it, stands back up)* I can't imagine why, I've never felt saner in my life. *(Gathers her document case and cloak)* Where do I stay ..?

WILLIE: Top of the house, will I show you?

MAUD: No need.

She leaves. Willie sits on in silence; puts the hand she kissed to his lips; kisses the kiss. His eyes close. Sudden sounds of laughter, a man's voice, a woman's, beyond the window. Shot through glass of garden, orchard, fence as before, as if in his point of view. The pair of young lovers drift slowly into frame as before, but now in late 19th Century dress.

His face, a thin smile on the lips, savouring what he conjures behind the lids.

Moving to

mute images as dreamed *of young Maud and Willie (1891; in their mid-20s) out by the fence, the summer house in the background. They stand side by side, looking out over sea. Willie grabs little looks at her, perilously overboard already.*

Sound bleeds abruptly in.

MAUD: There is magic here. Spirit. I feel it. *(Straightens a glove)* Can't be done, Willie, I can stay a few days longer, but I must get back to Paris …

Moving to

INT. ATTIC ROOM. AFT/EVE.

Tightening shot of Maud's face, restless, dozing, dreaming, on the red counterpane, typescript pages of her memoirs spread around her.

Moving back to

dream again*, Howth Head.*

WILLIE: Must? Who says so? No, you choose.

MAUD: Oh God, Willie, you're such a boy. Look.

WILLIE: No!

A gull screams on the wind. He walks away from her, stands at the cliff's edge.

MAUD: Don't spoil this day, Willie. I told you when we met: I took a vow on my father's grave to make my life's work the freeing of Ireland …

WILLIE: In <u>Paris</u>?

MAUD: Yes! There are people there who have Ireland's interests.

WILLIE: There are people **here**, Maud, a movement you can help lead, and I'll be at your side, every inch of the …

MAUD: Willie, **here** there's a warrant out for my arrest, helping evicted tenants get back their rightful homes is against the law. I'm no use to Ireland in a British gaol …

She turns, begins to walk back to the house. Moving to

INT. STUDY.

*Close shot of Willie, tranced, reliving every word. Beyond the window, the young Willie calls after her: **Maud. Maud.***

dream again:

Willie calls on. She turns to look back at him.

MAUD: I **must**, Willie.

WILLIE: Then I must come with you.

MAUD: To do what?

WILLIE: To share the work. To keep you from harm. To …

MAUD: No. Absolutely not. Your work is here.

WILLIE: *(Loud)* Not if you're not, it isn't. *(She turns away again, headed for the house. He shouts after her)* Is there another? Back there in Paris? Is there? Is there ..? Maud! Answer me …

His voice tails on the wind. The image hovers, the sound fades. A gentle knocking sets up, house acoustic.

WILLIE: *(Voice over, from the trance)* You lied, Maud. And in your book you lie still, there **was** another and you had already borne his child …

Moving to

INT. ATTIC GUEST ROOM. LIGHT FADING.

Maud bursts from sleep, sweating, disturbed. Grows slowly aware of the gentle knocking. Gathers.

MAUD: Who is it?

JANE: It's Jane, mum, Mrs Sweeney.

MAUD: Come.

JANE: *(Appearing)* … come to light your lamps.

MAUD: Please.

She crosses to light the mantels; slim, younger than Sweeney, oddly pretty. Maud sits on the edge of the bed, struggling to recover.

JANE: You alright, mum?

MAUD: Thank you, I'm fine.

JANE: *(gazing at the unpacked dress on wardrobe door)* Ach, such a beautiful thing, so it is. *(Leaving)* Dinner's on the way …

Maud smiles her thanks. Stands. Dips to wash her face in the waterbowl. Looks at herself in the tiny wallmirror.

The Burmese gong begins to hum from across the stairhead, low, steady. She crosses to the doorway, stares at the door to Willie's workroom.

JANE: *(stopped at crook of stair)* Pay it no heed, mum. Ye'll come to no harm, long as ye stay this side o' the door.

MAUD: Is he in there ..?

JANE: Below, mum. I just woke him.

EXT. LAMPLIT VERANDAH, OVERLOOKING SEA. LATE EVENING.

Sweeney carries a bowl of fruit to the makeshift dinner table, begins to gather the remains of the meal. Maud and Willie sit in silence across the table. She wears the beautiful black dress; Willie, light, alert, recovered, shines in a pale linen suit and red cravat.

MAUD: Please tell your wife the hare was wonderful, Mr Sweeney.

SWEENEY: So I will, milady.

He moves off.

WILLIE: *(Calling after him)* Coffee in the parlour, if ye please. *(To Maud)* Sligo Hare, it was bloody chicken …

He offers more wine, Maud caps her glass with her hand. They look at each other for a moment. He holds up his glass.

WILLIE: You look. Magnificent.

MAUD: Thank you. You look pretty fetching yourself.

WILLIE: Yes, I'll make a fine corpse.

MAUD: Do stop it, Willie. *(He grins at her, an impish boy again)* You'll see us all out.

She shivers. He gets up, places her shawl across her shoulders, moves to the rail, stares out at the glistening sound. She searches for a cigarette.

WILLIE: There is magic here. Spirit. *(She stops, flame to tip)* I feel it. *(Turns to look at her)* Yes?

MAUD: What are you up to, Willie? What about the book ..?

WILLIE: Forget the book, Maud, it's not the book.

MAUD: *(Fast to anger)* The hell it's not the book.

WILLIE: I mispoke, forgive me, I …

MAUD: Forget the book? *(Tough, deliberate)* I need the money, Willie, I'm the only breadwinner back there and drowning in a sea of dependent family and friends, I've had nothing but grief from the publishers, they're terrified someone will take out a libel action against it, you must have noticed the misnamings and misdatings I've had to resort to, if you don't give your agreement they'll toss it on the scrapheap … What do you mean it's not the book!

She stubs her cigarette, angry, upset. He returns to the table. Takes an unsealed envelope from his pocket, places it on the table in front of her.

MAUD: What's this?

WILLIE: Take a look.

She takes out the letter. Reads it.

WILLIE: I've carried that around for weeks. Will we go in?

MAUD: Wait. I thought the book was the reason I was here, if it's never been a problem ..?

WILLIE: It's the book disturbs me, Maud. Not its publication. *(She frowns)* Come, you'll catch a chill.

He leads her in, past Mrs Sweeney lighting the library mantels, to the parlour across the hall. Sweeney's there, tabling the coffee tray by the peat fire. Willie waves her to an armchair facing his; sits. Sweeney makes to pour.

WILLIE: Thank you, we can manage.

SWEENEY: *(Showing him the bottle)* Pills.

WILLIE: Yes yes. *(Reaches to pour. Sweeney stands firm. Willie takes the proferred pills and water glass. Tosses them back. Hands Sweeney the glass. Sweeney leaves.)* Bah! *(He scrapes the pills from under his tongue, throws them on the fire)* Damned things.

MAUD: What are they for?

WILLIE: Blood pressure.

MAUD: Is that wise?

WILLIE: Wise? I think so.

They sip their coffee in silence for a moment.

MAUD: *(The letter in her hand)* So I'm free to send your agreement? The book can go ahead ..?

WILLIE: Absolutely.

MAUD: Shuh! That's a relief. I thought I was going to have to spend the whole weekend fighting you.

WILLIE: Wouldn't be the first time. *(He digs a hand into a metal bowl of dark powder on the table)* Remember this?

He throws it onto the glowing peat. A flame bursts up, a curl of thick oily smoke floats out into the room.

MAUD: Mmm …

He nods, she smiles, shakes her head. He reaches for more.

MAUD: Enough. I'd prefer to keep my wits about me, at least until I know what the hell I'm doing here. Are you going to tell me? I mean if it's not my book.

WILLIE: It is the book, Maud, it is.

MAUD: Then kindly tell me how.

WILLIE: I'll try. *(He gets up, paces, hands on the move, gathering. She watches)* Some months back, I reached a … defining moment. Wait … *(He riffs through a roll-top desk, finds a leather-bound diary, looks for his page)* I got up one morning, full of the future, sat calmly down at my desk and wrote … *(Finds it)* '*I know for certain now that my time will not be long. In two or three weeks I will begin to write my most fundamental thoughts and my work will be over. It seems to me that I have found what I wanted …*' See, The last entry. Next day, the very next day, your book dropped onto my mat and proved me wrong. You do have that knack, Maud. From the first time I set eyes on you all those years ago, you brought into my life the sound as of a Burmese gong, an overpowering and unstemmable tumult, a sound that never left it. And here you were again, there on the mat, humming like a star through space, like a flame to the soles of my feet. Even now, at the end, bags packed, work done, set to go, your knuckle on the door, your hand on the latch, and suddenly I fill with doubt, glimpse something else I must know, something there and not there, blowing through my head and heart and shaking to its root the peace I felt I'd found … I can not die like this. Will not. I will not leave with less than everything. *(He examines her face)* How can I bring you to understanding? How can I bring myself?

He paces on, hands carving air, struggling for meaning. The phone bell starts whirring across the hall. Neither notices. It's picked up.

MAUD: Sit, Willie. You'll wear a hole in the carpet. And another in your brain-pan, I shouldn't wonder. *(He resumes his seat)* It's the book and not the book, something there and not there, you want me to understand but don't understand it yourself, you don't make it easy, friend.

WILLIE: I know. If it weren't so grave, it'd be really quite comical …

She blinks, prepares to laugh; sees Sweeney in the doorway.

SWEENEY: That's the phone thing there … *(Willie swipes the arm of his chair in frustration; begins levering himself upright again. Sweeney waits till he's almost there)* For milady.

MAUD: Who on earth ..?

She frowns her way to the library. Willie stays on his feet; scowls.

WILLIE: Who is it, did they say?

SWEENEY: Didn't say, didn't ask. I'm off to my bed.

WILLIE: Take those lamps away, will ye. *(Sweeney squints at him, unmoving)* I don't need them.

SWEENEY: Will I just turn 'em off ..?

WILLIE: Take them.

Sweeney removes the two oil lamps, leaves heavily. Willie broods, takes another hand of incense, sprinkles it on a glowing chunk of peat spilled onto the hearth, moves out into the hall to look through the open doorway at Maud on the phone. Her voice just fails to carry the distance.

INT. LIBRARY.

MAUD: *(At phone)* Wait … *(She searches pencil and paper; settles for Willie's copy of her MS)* Say the name again. *(writes it down on the cover)* Yes, I know the family. And who gave him my number? Ahunh. And you told him I was here for the weekend … Right, give me a second. *(She lays the receiver down, paces a little, working stuff out. Becomes aware of Willie in the hallway, watching her. Returns to phone.)* Look, I think it's best you stay out of it, love, if he does turn up, I suppose I'll handle it, the poor devil. Mm. Thanks.

She places the phone down, establishes Willie's gone, finds a piece of notepaper in a drawer, folds and places it in her bag, returns to

INT. PARLOUR

MAUD: My son. His boy's running a fever.

She takes in the darkened room, the smoulder of lapsed peat on the hearth, resumes her armchair.

WILLIE: They'll cope?

MAUD: I should think so. What happened to the lamps?

WILLIE: Sweeney has them. He's up to bed.

She settles back, runs a finger along a coil of incense held in thick air above her head. Silence.

MAUD: Who says you're dying, Willie?

WILLIE: I do.

MAUD: No physicians, specialists ..?

WILLIE: How would they know?

MAUD: Oh God, I bet your doctors love you.

WILLIE: About as much as I love their bills.

She chuckles. Can't stop, the incense beginning to kick in.

WILLIE: I said something funny? I hate the bastards. They charged me a fortune for an operation to restore my vitality a few years back, monkey glands, couldn't do without it, they said, horseshit of course, didn't restore a thing … Unless you count the more or less permanent erection I was left with for the next two years, fat lot of good that was to a man with work to do.

She chuckles on, he relents at last, acknowledges the joke he's being, laughs with her. They wind down towards silence. Look at each other through the wisping smoke.

MAUD: You wouldn't have a drop of the pure stuff, would you, Willie?

WILLIE: I have something much better. Will I fetch it?

MAUD: Much better than whiskey? I'm not sure I'm ready for that. *(She gets up, wanders the room, sees remembered pics, remembered people)* You've been in my dreams for weeks. And here today too. But you know that, don't you.

Is that all part of this? *(She comes back to sit on the floor by the fire, her back against her chair, lithe arms around supple knees; looks at him for a moment)* You're such a bloody ringmaster, you know. Mr Yeats' Magic Circus. Introducing Maud the Wonder Horse, who will prance and skip to order and step through hoops of fire for your delight and edification … You could have just asked, Willie. I would have come. You didn't need to put the wind up me about the book or walk around my head muttering instructions. I would have come.

Willie watches her throughout, face, hair, hand, the rucked skirt, the black silk glint of ankles below it.

WILLIE: Would you? I couldn't be sure. Things had grown so cold. Why should you want to spend your time helping a reactionary old … fascist did ye call me? … who sold his freedom for a pot of fame and betrayed the cause of Ireland ..?

MAUD: *(Simple)* Because you're Willie. And I'm Maud.

WILLIE: You put me to shame. Forgive me.

He reaches for her hand. Puts it to his lips. She runs a finger through his flop of hair.

MAUD: Will you sleep now?

WILLIE: Sleep? Gave it up long since. I need to go on with this, are you tired ..?

MAUD: Not at all. But I need cigarettes, I have some in my room.

WILLIE: Will I fetch them?

MAUD: *(Up on her feet)* No no. You fetch that stuff you spoke of. It's beginning to look like a session.

She gathers her things, leaves. He follows to the door, watches her climb the stair, crosses to the library.

INT. STAIRWAY LANDING.

Maud heads for her room. Faint sounds from a back-bedroom. She turns onto the second flight, listens. Hears the faint rhythmic insistence of bedsprings, voiced pleasure: the Sweeneys at love.

JANE: *(off, from within, laughing)* … Holy Christ, Mr Sweeney, you still have yer sweaty old **socks** on.

SWEENEY: *(off, chuckling)* I do, I do …

Maud smiles, moves on.

INT. LIBRARY.

*Willie finds what he needs at his desk: notepad, fountain pen. Crosses to the mantelpiece, lifts the pot cat, screws off its head, removes a small package, puts it in his coatpocket. Remembers he needs his copy of Maud's memoirs, collects it from the desk. Sees the name she pencilled on the cover: **Finnegan**. Studies it. Leaves for the stairs.*

INT. ATTIC ROOM.

Maud transfers a fresh supply of cigarettes from packet to monogrammed silver case. Takes pencil and notepaper from her bag, hears a creak on the stair, crosses to close the door, returns to paper and pen, begins to write:

'To whom it may concern

Mr Finnegan'

She thinks a moment, presses on.

The gong begins to hum across the stairhead. She listens a moment. Finishes the note. Gathers her things. Leaves to go back downstairs.

INT. STAIRHEAD.

The workroom door lies open, the room half-lit. She moves a touch closer, peers inside. A small fire burns in the grate. Light splashes the room through the sea-facing windows: red, black; red, black; red, black; the Bailey Lighthouse at work. She edges forward a little, scans the empty room. Locates the Burmese gong, still humming. Prepares to leave.

WILLIE: *(From within)* Come. We'll work here. Almost there.

She scans the room again, looks behind the door: nothing.

MAUD: Where are you?

WILLIE: Come.

She moves warily in, following the source of the voice towards a far corner of the room.

WILLIE: *(Behind her)* See.

She turns sharply. He steps out from behind a lacquered folding screen, face gleaming in the Bailey light, a small fine-wrought hookah in his hands. Carries it to the fireplace, waves her to the chaise longue precisely placed before it. She drifts after him, wary; lays her bag on the chaise.

WILLIE: *(Kneeling to the work)* I'll need a little tobacco. *(He takes out a penknife and the package, begins unwrapping it)* May I?

He reaches for her bag, she rescues it just in time, hands him the silver cigarette case. The unfinished letter lies beneath her fingers at the top of the bag.

MAUD: What is it?

WILLIE: *(Holding it up; a 1/2lb ball.)* Hashish. From Nepal. A Swami taught me how to use it. See the white stripes? Opium. Enfolded, see. Better than whiskey.

He works on, laying thin strips of hash on top of the bed of tobacco.

MAUD: Better for what, Willie?

WILLIE: The journey. We are upon experiments, my love. Sit, won't you. I'm getting a crick …

He moves off into the room, gathering what he needs, charged, vital, in his element. She watches him, rounds the chaise, delays the sit.

MAUD: This. Journey, Willie. What is it, exactly?

He returns laden, begins laying things on the coffee table by the fire: a large painted metal bowl, an uncorked champagne bottle, matches, tapers, a Tarot box.

WILLIE: I do wish you would sit, Maud, you're <u>so</u> bloody tall, you know.

She smiles, removes his copy of the memoir from the chaise, lays it on the coffee table, sits.

WILLIE: *(Emptying bottle into bowl)* … Seawater. Irish. What is this journey exactly? I can't exactly say. A journey is not only the journey we take but also the journey we make. You used to know that. *(Sprinkles a pinch of tiny dried flowers onto the water. Lowers the oil lamp, lights a candle here and there, peers back into the bowl).* See.

She looks, their faces quite close. In the bowl, the dried flowers are beginning to swell. He shakes it a little, the water dances.

MAUD: Where are we going, Willie?

WILLIE: Wherever you take us, my love.

MAUD: In search of what?

WILLIE: The truth your book glimpsed and shied away from. The truth I know I've lost.

MAUD: I'm not sure I'm up to it, Willie. It's half a lifetime since.

WILLIE: The power is in you still. I know it.

He lights a taper, fires the bubble-pipe, draws on it, turns it to her. She stares at it. He moves to a gramophone, winds it taut, lays a record on the turntable, sets the needle hissing.

She looks at the pipe, the bowl; the manuscript. **Finnegan** *burns up at her from the cover.*

WILLIE: *(Returning to a chair)* Time to go.

Maud takes a hit, blinks as it hits her; lies back across the chaise, like a patient in analysis. Willie shakes the bowl again. Sits back in his chair, as if preparing for take-off. Close shot of the water, swaying, lapping.

The poet's voice speaks out from the gram.

> '…Those masterful images because complete
> Grew in pure mind, but out of what began?
> A mound of refuse or the sweepings of a street,
> Old kettles, old bottles, and a broken can …

Maud's face, eyes closing. Willie's lips, drawing smoke through a gurgle of water, face burning in Bailey light. The water in the bowl, growing choppy, agitated.

Old iron, old bones, old rags, that raving slut
Who keeps the till.

Long still shot of the moonlit sea in Dublin Bay. Long still shot of the headland summerhouse, windows lit against the dark.

Now that my ladder's gone,
I must lie down where all the ladders start,

Close shot of Maud's face, eyes bobbling beneath the lids, en route.

In the foul rag-and-bone shop of the heart.'

Willie's face, head back, eyes closed, en route; the water dancing; the ridged moonlit sea, frame slowing to a frozen silvered abstraction, a sort of seascreen for their shared.

VISION

EXT.DAY.GRAVEYARD. S.ENGLAND, 1871.

Mute slowed bleached shots of a country funeral. Upper class family mourners, high church ceremonial, dignified restraint much in evidence.

Shot of Tommy Gonne, late 30s, tall, goodlooking, heavily moustached, in the dress uniform of an Army captain. He holds a weeping three-year old daughter, Kathleen, in his left arm. We pan down his right arm to reveal the five-year Maud clutching his hand, watching with a hard, detached fascination as her mother's coffin is lowered.

MAUD: *(Over, from trance)* Never be afraid of anything, he said. Even death …

EXT. DAY. DONEGAL. 1882.

Mute bleached shots of Ascendancy Ireland. We pick up members of a houseparty riding fields and bridleways, Tommy and Maud (16) among them. The group's progress is halted on the outskirts of a small village by an eviction. A battering ram splinters the barred front door, men move in, an ancient woman is carried out on a mattress, a mother and baby follow.

WILLIE: *(Over, from trance)* I can't hear, I need words …

A small band of protesting Landleaguers spot the group, rush forward to shout and wave their banners at the landowner who leads them. R.I.C. men drag them off, clearing the way. Other villagers tip their hats. Maud watches, horror growing on her face. The landowner says something to a companion; they bark into laughter as he leads the group imperiously on.

Maud stays on, drawn by the scene. Sound bleeds slowly in. The riders' laughter floats back across the eviction men, now busy smashing roof and windows.

INT. EVENING. DEBUTANTES' BALL, ST PATRICK'S HALL, DUBLIN. 1883.

Wildtrack sound covers slowed beached shots of a court photographer preparing a group picture. Through his lens we see the group finding its positions: Edward,

Prince of Wales, his idiot son the Duke of Clarence, Tommy Gonne in Colonel's dress uniform and Maud (17), in shimmering dress, water-lily train and ostrich-feather fan. Edward banishes his idiot son to the edges, insists Maud stands next to him. Tommy and Maud share a smiling unimpressed look. The lens follows the movement of personnel, seeking the compositional moment; catches the Prince's hand casually groping the young woman's arm and hip.

The picture is ready: a magnesium flash; the image resolves into the monochrome photograph we saw in Willie's workroom (p.5). Trail **Dead March** *from Saul; move to*

EXT. DAY. DUBLIN QUAYS, NORTH WALL, 1886.

March continues wildtracked over Tommy's funeral procession. Maud (19) and Kathleen head the mourners following the gun-carriage bearing the coffin to the British boat waiting to take her father's body back to England. Thin sifting rain soaks the cortège and the military Guard of Honour. Tommy's sister, Mary, Comtesse de la Sizeranne, tries to shelter her two nieces with a huge umbrella. Maud's face gives little away, 'the Colonel's daughter', but the grief and loss run deep. The procession stops at the North Wall, the coffin's slowmarched on board. Maud comforts her distraught sister; is suddenly taken by a paroxysm of coughing. Aunt Mary hands her her kerchief, the fit subsides, the kerchief's handed back, flecked with blood. Aunt Mary notes it, eyes grim.

MAUD: *(Over, whispered, from trance) Oh Tommy, Tommy, I miss you still, I have never stopped missing you.*

WILLIE: *(Ditto) On, on … Where now?*

EXT. DAY. CHATEAU SPA, ROYAT, FRANCE, 1887.

A sweltering summer day. The chateau shimmers in the heat. Thunder in nearby Puy-de-Dôme.

WILLIE: *(Over, from trance) Ah. Lover boy!* <u>*Now*</u> *to the foul rag-and-bone shop of the heart …*

MAUD: *(Over) No, Willie, I won't have you pushing me …*

The image begins to break down, as if resolving back to frozen seascreen.

WILLIE: *(Over) Please, I'm sorry, you're quite right …*

A band sets up. The image resumes. Gives way to

EXT. DAY. TREE-LINED PROMENADE, CHATEAU GROUNDS.

Five women seated on a long bench under trees fanning themselves with identical great black fans. Spa clients, of similar wealth and ease, pass slowly before them, hobbling, wheelchaired or whatever. Maud (20), recovering but still pale, sits to one side of Aunt Mary, her sister Kathleen by her side. A French friend and her daughter make up the group.

A tall cultivated man, late thirties, elegant, heavily moustached, approaches the group, his male secretary in tow. He greets Aunt Mary's friend; is introduced to the bench.

Close shot of him brushing Maud's hand with his lips; Maud's face, looking up at him, seeing her father's lineaments at once in the man before her.

MILLEVOIE: Lucien Millevoie, Mamselle. Enchanté.

He moves on to Kathleen. Maud's eyes stay with him, drawn; take him in.

WILLIE: *(Over, from trance)* My God, look at you. Right away! Hot, instant. You cannot see the wolf for the peacock.

MAUD: *(Over, ditto; tough)* We can end the journey right here if you want, Willie. None of this is easy …

WILLIE: *(Over, ditto)* I'm quiet, I'm quiet.

The five ladies stand, the men accompany them towards the Chateau's Residential Quarters. The band plays on.

INT. MID-EVENING. AUNT MARY'S SUITE.

Maud stands at the french windows, looking out. Thunder, close. Jags of lightning turn her face spectral. Behind her, preparations are under way for retirement.

We see what she's looking at: Millevoie under a lamp-lit tree in the avenue, reading a book.

Aunt Mary approaches, Kathleen on her arm.

AUNT MARY: *(On the approach)* Come, child, to bed. Sleep is beauty, sleep is health, as my third husband the Count was wont to say. Boring, my dear, but true. Much like my third husband.

Maud turns half-guiltily, places her back to the pane to block the view.

MAUD: I'm waiting for the storm, Aunt. It's almost here. Ten minutes. I promise.

AUNT MARY: Not a second more.

They kiss, Maud hugs Kathleen goodnight, they fade into the darkening recesses of the Salle. The storm outside begins to break.

Maud returns her gaze to the man across the way. He's gone. She scans the promenade. Opens the French windows, steps out onto the canopied balcony. Rain slashes across the parkland; lightning; Wagnerian thunder. She grows powerfully drawn to it; watches the rosebed below fill with dashed petals; stretches an arm out beyond the canopy to feel the rain.

A hand reaches up from below to touch it. She starts. Sees Millevoie on the lawn directly below the balcony. Water pours down his already soaked head and body.

MAUD: Qu'est-ce que vous faîtes, Monsieur?

MILLEVOIE: *(Serviceable English)* I was waiting for the storm. And you?

MAUD: Moi aussi. C'est splendide, parfait, non?

MILLEVOIE: Splendid, yes, perfect no. **You** are perfect, Maud Gonne.

The storm's moving on. They stare at each other in the growing calm.

MILLEVOIE: My friend Mme Feline tells me you fight to throw the British out of Ireland.

MAUD: The same lady tells me you run a newspaper dedicated to smashing the alliance between France and England.

He turns away, scans the dripping parkland. Mist rises from the hot earth.

MILLEVOIE: There is much to say. Will you walk with me?

MAUD: I might.

He looks at her. Reaches for her hand. Kisses the palm.

MILLEVOIE: Perhaps we should build a new alliance, France and Ireland. Une entente cordiale?

Long shot of the chateau wing. Millevoie holds his arms up, Maud climbs the balcony rail and eases down into them. Dissolving to

Mute abstract images of bodies coupling, Maud's, Millevoie's, covering the early years of the relationship. They fuck on stone floors, rugs, tables, desks, beds, in grass, carriages. Their sex is never gentle, giving; often it's brutally direct, a struggle for dominance; frequently it ends in recrimination, coolness.

MAUD: *(Through this, from trance)* Impossible to say if I ever loved him, love was never a word we shared. But for years he drew me terribly, long after I had begun to despise him.

WILLIE: *(Over, from trance; pained)* All this, all this, even before

EXT. NIGHT. BEDFORD PARK, LONDON, 1889.

Sounds of heart-beat over mute shots of Maud (22) stepping from a hansom cab outside 3 Blenheim Road, the modest brick villa rented by the Yeats family. Her stunningly distinctive Parisian couture gives out at the feet, which are unexplainedly slippered. She stands the hansom by, searches for the house, rings the bell. The door's opened.

WILLIE: *(Over, from trance)* Ah, the troubling of my life begins.

INT. NIGHT. SITTING ROOM.

Heart-beat sounds continue and quicken over mute images of arrival, greetings, introductions. Willie's father, JB, comes forward to greet her, introduces his excited teenage daughters Lily and Lolly, sons Jack (16) and Willie (23), shows her a chair. Lily and Lolly, agog, pour the tea and hand it round. Jack sits on the carpet by his father's chair, eyes fixed on her. Willie sits in the half-light by the window, characteristically outside the family loop, flicking fascinated glances at her through the dark sweep of hair masking his eyes.

WILLIE: *(Over, from trance)* What is that sound?

MAUD: *(Ditto)* I believe it's your heart, Willie.

The heart-beat fades, full sync sound bleeds in. JB has resumed his dominant chair by the Adam fireplace.

JB: ... Well now, Miss Gonne, what a pleasure. (*She smiles, takes out her Russian cigarettes*) You'll forgive the excitement, but your reputation does somewhat precede you, John O'Leary wrote me only last week of your most recent exploits, some of which he does not approve, I should add, though he does regard you still as his most hopeful recruit ...

MAUD: You mean my work with the Land League?

JB: I do. He believes the status of Ireland will not be materially altered by individual acts of violent resistance, sticks and staves and the like, on the part of evicted tenants, and on the whole I believe he is right.

MAUD: I'm sorry to hear it, Mr Yeats. You know of a peaceful way of ending British Rule, do you?

JB: I'm a painter, Miss Gonne, not a politician, but it does seem seriously wrong-headed to help the Irish peasant by asking him to wave his shelalagh at a rifle, and irresponsible too, since he will only end up getting shot or serving a long sentence in a British gaol.

MAUD: Mr Yeats, I am not a member of the Land League and cannot speak for its tactics any more than you or John O'Leary can. But last month I led a torchlit procession of more than a thousand on Limerick Castle Hall in order to negotiate a reduction in rents with the Landlords, in which I should say we were successful. Now, do you think it was my silver tongue or the sight and sound of that unprecedented throng – with their sticks and staves and torches – that won us the day?

She lights a cigarette, composed, unafraid, smiles at the dumbstruck girls on the sofa. Willie's dark eyes burn at her through the hair; he's wholly taken.

JB: Well, having met you at last, Miss Gonne, I think it might well have been a little of each. (*His daughters chuckle, relieved he hasn't exploded.*) More tea, Lolly.

Lolly takes charge. Willie finds a bowl for Maud's ash. She takes it with a smile, widens her eyes to look at him. Willie swallows hard, fearful of her scrutiny, too shy to speak.

MAUD: You're the poet of the family, am I right?

WILLIE: Well, yes, I have written some verse.

MAUD: Mr O'Leary mentioned a small volume you'd had published.

WILLIE: Quite small, yes. Well, very small.

MAUD: I have a project I'd like to discuss with you, perhaps we could have dinner one evening while I'm in town?

WILLIE: Dinner? Certainly. I'd like that very much.

MAUD: Good.

He edges awkwardly back to his chair, dismissed.

MAUD: *(Focused; on)* Mr Yeats, I am in London to present a petition to the British Home Secretary demanding the release of all Irish political prisoners. Your name on it would greatly help the cause.

JB: Political prisoners? I wasn't aware there were such men, who are they, pray?

MAUD: The Dynamiters, Mr Yeats. Eighteen patriots rotting in English gaols, I have visited them all and sworn to work for their release …

JB: Miss Gonne, I will have nothing to do with violence, to me these men are criminals aiming terror at the innocent.

MAUD: Then I will not press you, sir. Though your description would seem to fit the British in Ireland rather the better than the men I refer to.

JB: You are young, Miss Gonne, and you will learn …

Sound fades. The exchange continues mute a little longer. Close shot of Willie, marvelling at her.

WILLIE: *(Over, from trance) God, Maud, you hit my life like a bomb.*

Sounds of a doorbell. Moving to

INT. EBURY ST. MANSIONS, LONDON. NEXT EVENING.

Shot of oak door from inside the apartment. Maud appears in shot to open it. Willie shines on the doormat like a beautiful boy.

MAUD: Ah Mr Yeats, you're early, do come in.

WILLIE: Thank you. I brought you this.

She takes his slim volume of verse. Opens it. Reads his inscription.

MAUD: That's very flattering, thank you. As a matter of fact I went out this morning and bought a copy for myself. Come through.

He follows her into her drawing room. Blinks at the eccentric menagerie it houses: Dagda the Wolfhound, four persian cats, two doves in cages, Chaperon the Gibraltar Monkey. Notes she wears her slippers again.

MAUD: *(Indicating a table)* Have a seat.

She brings a lamp, sets it on the table between them, splashing light on his face. Studies him steadily for some time.

WILLIE: *(trying for calm; unnerved)* What?

MAUD: Forgive me, I was looking for something … an aura, shape … it was very strong the other night when we met.

WILLIE: Ah. And tonight?

MAUD: No. Not this evening. I read your poems, by the way. They're very fine. It's a very pure talent you have.

WILLIE: You think so?

MAUD: I do.

He looks at her, she holds his eyes, he looks away, too scared to go on looking, out of his depth.

MAUD: Pity you haven't yet found something important to write about, but that will come, you're young still, what are ye, twenty?

WILLIE: Twenty-four.

MAUD: Really? You should eat more. Where shall we dine? There's an Irish Fish Bar in Soho …

She collects her cloak and bag.

WILLIE: Ah, I see, I thought we were to eat here …

MAUD: Here? Whatever gave you that idea? I don't cook …

WILLIE: Of course, erm. Is it expensive, this er, I came without …

MAUD: A few shillings. I'll pay mine … *(She watches him fiddling through his pockets)* How much have you?

WILLIE: *(Squirming)* Sixpence ..?

MAUD: Come, I have enough.

WILLIE: No no, I can't allow that.

MAUD: We have to eat, my friend.

WILLIE: I'm really not hungry.

MAUD: Nonsense. Come along, I know just the place …

Dagda and Chaperon prepare to go with her, she shoos them away. Willie follows in her tailstream.

INT. NIGHT. KERBSIDE CAB STATION, HAMMERSMITH.

Maud and Willie stand in line at the Food Hatch, waiting for their penny pie and gravy. Cabbies nosh away on benches at the sides of the long narrow station, eyeing the pair: clothes, class, slippers.

Maud leads Willie down the hut, nodding and smiling at the cabbies. Willie follows her, plates in hand, deeply uncomfortable. They find a place to sit.

Willie sets to at once, ravenous. She watches him; smiles.

MAUD: *(Over, from trance)* I always loved the boy in you, Willie. Is any of this helping?

WILLIE: *(Over, ditto)* Hush. Let the will move of itself and we will find it.

Willie's finishing off the gravy with a chunk of bread.

MAUD: Best penny pie in London. *(He grunts agreement, busy)* Have another. *(He shakes his head)* Go on, I had a huge lunch at the House of Commons, working my charm on those unspeakable Home Rulers.

WILLIE: No no, you must be hungry.

MAUD: I'm not.

WILLIE: *(Eyes it, takes it)* If you're sure. It just happens to be my fasting day, I
eat nothing until dinner on Thursdays.

MAUD: Is that a spiritual thing ..?

WILLIE: No, it's a way of buying the books I need. And good training for the sort
of material future I can expect from a life as a poet. For that is the life I
intend to live.

MAUD: *(Squinting at him)* I'm damned.

WILLIE: What?

MAUD: The aura. It's back.

WILLIE: Ah. Describe it. Does it have colour?

MAUD: Green. It's green. Mm.

*He lays the plate down, takes out a notebook and pencil, jots it all down. Puts a
circle round it. Lays a large ? against it. Resumes his second pie.*

MAUD: Why green, do you think?

WILLIE: I'll need to give it thought.

A cabbie arrives at their bench, takes off his hat.

CABBIE: Evnin, Miss, wondered if ye needed a hansom, I'm just about on my
way.

MAUD: Thank you, Albert, I think I'll walk this evening. But if you'd care to call
at Ebury Street around ten, I think we could find you a fare.

CABBIE: Much obliged, mum.

WILLIE: *(Amazed)* Do you know everyone in London?

MAUD: I know Albert, I've been his fare often enough.

WILLIE: Do you feel no fear?

MAUD: None. Should I?

He shakes his head, shrugs, aware of her utter otherness.

EXT. SOHO STREETS. LAMPLIT.

*They walk in silence, through populous pavements. Willie stops at a pet shop
window, gazes in at ping pong balls rising and falling on jets of water.*

MAUD: What are you thinking of?

WILLIE: I'm thinking of Ireland. Sligo, actually. Innisfree. Where I grew up. Were
you ever there?

MAUD: No. Perhaps you'll take me one day.

WILLIE: You mean that?

She smiles, puts her arm in his, walks him on.

MAUD: *(On the fade)* You're going to have to learn to trust me, Willie. When I say something, I usually mean it.

WILLIE: Miss Gonne.

MAUD: Maud.

EXT. EBURY STREET. NIGHT.

A church clock strikes ten as they approach her apartment block. Albert stands by his Hansom at the kerb. Maud mounts the steps to the front door. Willie watches, bursting to follow.

MAUD: We will be friends, will we?

WILLIE: Yes. May I write you?

MAUD: You may. So long as you write for Ireland too.

She unlocks the door, turns.

MAUD: My friend has fourpence, Albert. Will that see him to Bedford Park?

Albert frowns, certain it won't. She gives him a covert nod, he reads the sign.

ALBERT: Not a problem. Ready when you are, sir.

Sounds fade. Willie boards the cab. Maud waves from the open door.

WILLIE: *(Over, from trance)* The slippers, Maud. Why did you wear the slippers …?

MAUD: *Can't you guess, Willie?*

INT. DAY. PARIS APARTMENT. BEDROOM. 1890.

Mute images of Maud in the throes of childbirth. A physician and a midwife work hard to deliver the obdurate Georges. Millevoie stands by the window, close to tears; turns at a call from the bed; sees the boy held up in the midwife's hands.

INT. DAY. PARIS APARTMENT. MAUD'S 'IRLANDE LIBRE' OFFICE. 1891.

*Maud works at her cornerdesk, dressed for travel, bags around her. The walls by her desk are covered in cuttings of her letters and articles, hundreds of them, under a red-and-black sign: **Irlande Libre**. From time to time she turns to look at baby Georges at the wetnurse's breast in the adjoining nursery.*

Doorbell. She stands, peers through the window, sees the carriage arrived on the street below, gathers her things, crosses to the nursery to have a last hug of the child, returns for her bags.

Millevoie in with cabman, whom he directs to carry her bags out. She tidies her desk. Millevoie watches

MILLEVOIE: *(Cool, polite)* How long will you be, do you know?

MAUD: *(Calm)* A month, I'm not sure, depends if I'm allowed to see the political prisoners.

MILLEVOIE: I must say I'd rather hoped motherhood might have tempered your romantic obsession with Ireland, but you are your own woman, I will not complain.

MAUD: Good. How's your wife?

A small silence.

MILLEVOIE: Not greatly changed. *(She's ready to leave)* Don't I get a kiss? *(She kisses his cheek, en route. He takes her arm, holds her back)* There are times I fancy you have other men in your life, over there. *(She looks at him coolly, says nothing)* But I'm sure you would not sleep with them. *(She moves to break the hold)* Unless of course there were some political advantage to be had.

She removes his hands from her arms.

MAUD: I will not grace that with comment, Lucien. Send for me at once if I'm needed.

The boy begins crying in the adjoining room. She listens, bites her lip; leaves.

EXT. DAY. ROWING BOAT. 1891

Mute images of oars on water, a slow dipping and rising.

WILLIE: *(Over, from trance, interest quickening)* Ah wait, what's this…?

The phone rings downstairs, is left unanswered, cuts.

WILLIE: *(Over, ditto)* Is it here? Is this it ..?

The image tilts to reveal the tiny island the boat's approaching.

MAUD: *(Over, ditto)* Ireland's Eye, Willie, don't you remember? Just after we'd buried Parnell?

WILLIE: *(Ditto; cooling)* Ach. For a moment it seemed, I don't know, close.

EXT. DAY. IRELAND'S EYE.

The boat lies moored on a shingle beach. A sea mile away, Howth Head, the summer house, the Bailey Lighthouse. Slow mazy track of the island, rock, bird, bracken, until we reach the pair on a high ledge overlooking the water.

WILLIE: *(Over, throughout, reading)*
    'When you are old and grey and full of sleep
    And nodding by the fire, take down this book,
    And slowly read, and dream of the soft look
    Your eyes had once, and of their shadows deep;
    How many loved your moments of glad grace,
    And loved your beauty with love false or true,
    But one man loved the pilgrim soul in you,
    And loved the sorrows of your changing face …'

The shot reaches them. Willie stands in shadow, reading from his notebook; Maud sits watching him.

WILLIE: There's another verse, I haven't got it right yet.

MAUD: It's beautiful.

WILLIE: It's for you. *(She says nothing, looks away.)* Do you feel the spirits here?

MAUD: Mm.

WILLIE: All Ireland's alive with them. I'd love to show you Sligo. How long can you stay?

MAUD: I don't know. I'm waiting for a letter.

He walks to the end of the ledge, hurls a stone into the sea, a brief freak of sulky frustration. Maud stands, gathers.

MAUD: What's wrong?

WILLIE: Nothing. *(Silence)* I'm writing a play for you. About Cathleen Ní Houlihan. I want you to play Cathleen.

MAUD: Brilliant. What a tremendous idea. We'll find a place in Dublin for it and call it the National Theatre of Ireland, what do you say?

WILLIE: I have to write it first, but yes.

She walks towards him, takes him in her arms, hugs him like a younger brother.

MAUD: Oh Willie, Willie, Willie, you're the best friend in all the world and I love you dearly.

Shot of Willie's face over her shoulder, wanting so much, daring so little.

Shot of the cliff, the ledge, the locked couple. Sound fades.

*EXT. DAY. HOWTH HEAD./**The dream reprised.***

They stand by the cliff's edge. She gazes at the hazing sea, the island they've just left. He waits for answer.

MAUD: There is magic here. Spirit. I feel it. *(Straightens a glove)* Can't be done, Willie, I can stay a few days longer, but I must get back …

WILLIE: Must? Who says so? No, you choose.

MAUD: Oh God, Willie, you're such a boy. Look.

WILLIE: No!

A gull screams on the wind. He walks away from her, stands at the cliff's edge.

MAUD: Don't spoil this day, Willie. I told you when we met: I took a vow on my father's grave to make my life's work the freeing of Ireland …

WILLIE: In <u>Paris</u>?

MAUD: Yes! There are people there who have Ireland's interests …

WILLIE: There are people **here**, Maud, a movement you can help lead, and I'll be at your side, every inch of the …

MAUD: Willie, **here** there's a warrant out for my arrest, helping evicted tenants get back their rightful homes is against the law. I'm no use to Ireland in a British gaol …

She turns, begins to walk back to the house. He watches a moment, calls after her: **Maud. Maud.**

MAUD: *(Turning, calling)* I **must**, Willie.

WILLIE: Then I must come with you.

MAUD: To do what?

WILLIE: To share the work. To keep you from harm. To …

MAUD: No. Absolutely not. Your work is here.

WILLIE: *(Loud)* Not if you're not, it isn't! *(She turns away again, headed for the house. He shouts after her)* Is there another? Back there in Paris? Is there? Is there ..? Maud! Answer me …

His voice tails on the wind. She heads for the summer house, lets herself into the porch. Picks up a letter from behind the door, opens it, begins to read.

Willie sprints up, breathless.

WILLIE: Forgive me, that was childish. *(Sees the pallor on her face, the fear in her eyes.)* What? What is it?

She looks at him, barely aware he's there.

MAUD: I have to leave at once …

Sound fades. She waves the letter as if in evidence, heads off up the stairs to her room. Willie's face, watching her leave his life again, powerless to stop her.

WILLIE: *(Over, from trance)* How you lied, Maud. There **was** another and you had already borne his child …

INT. PRIVATE VAULT, PARIS CEMETERY. 1894.

Mute images of Maud (27) letting herself in to the ornate stone vault. She locks the door behind her, crosses to the tomb in the middle of the floor, lays a bunch of roses on it.

MAUD: *(Over, from trance)* I did not lie, Willie. I simply concealed what could not be uttered. You've never been a woman, my friend, and nothing I've read of yours in fifty years suggests you have the faintest idea what it is to be one. Perhaps there'll come a time when women can speak their truth, but it was not then and it is not now.

The heavy door swings open, Millevoie stands there a moment, lit by the sun, searching for her in the dark space; relocks the door; walks, slow, deliberate, to the tomb.

MAUD: *(Over, from trance)* The boy was ill, meningitis, he died just after I got home, for many months I couldn't speak, or sleep, or hope …

WILLIE: *(Over, from trance)* And what's this ..?

Fade in full sound. Millevoie has arrived by the marble tomb.

MILLEVOIE: I had your letter. *(Glances around the vault)* What do you want of me?

MAUD: I want another child.

MILLEVOIE: *(Stunned)* Another child.

MAUD: Yes.

MILLEVOIE: *(Eyes her, thinks.)* Can we not talk of this somewhere el..?

MAUD: … It has to happen here, Lucien. *(She lays a hand on the brass plaque inset into the top of the tomb)* Here.

MILLEVOIE: Is this one of your spirit theories ..?

MAUD: Does it matter?

She lifts herself on to the marble tomb, stretches her long legs out in front of her, stares at him.

MAUD: Does it?

She lies back, draws up and parts her knees, pulls her skirt up to her middle.

He stares at her. Then at her groin. Sound fades.

EXT. DAY. CONVENT NEAR PARIS. 1896.

Mute shots of Maud (30), walking through trees with 3 year old daughter in the convent grounds.

WILLIE: *(Over, from trance)* … So all those questions you asked me about reincarnating the spirit of a dead child in the next one were on your own behalf, not a friend's … And that's Iseult.

Her carriage waits in the drive. The Mother Superior is at the top of the steps, ready to take the child from the mother.

A last long hugging kiss, Maud climbs into her carriage, waves her goodbye.

MAUD: *(Over, from trance)* You have it, Willie …

INT. EVENING. DRAWING ROOM, MAUD'S SUITE, NASSAU HOTEL, DUBLIN. 1897.

Maud (31) sits at a French window, staring at the darkening sky from the darkening room. She's pallid, eyes lifeless, cheeks tear-streaked. The small table by her chair is littered with medicines. Sudden raised voices in adjoining room; Mrs Old, her hired nurse, enters on the knock.

MRS OLD: There's a Mr Yeats outside, ma'am, I've told him till I'm blue in the face you're seeing no one.

MAUD: Ask him in, will you.

Mrs Old sniffs, turns, waves Willie forward, grudgingly announces him. Willie appears, a wholly transformed man, elegant, confident, stylish in corn-coloured suit and apricot cravat. He thrusts a bunch of roses into the Nurse's hands.

WILLIE: Put those in a vase, will you. And try to remember you're a hired assistant, not Supreme Leader of the Galaxy. *(She leaves, less than pleased)* I came as soon as I got your card …

MAUD: I sent it a week back …

WILLIE: I've been away. If you'd let me know you were coming.

MAUD: I thought I'd surprise you. Come and sit down. Why are you so angry?

WILLIE: I haven't heard from you in an age, you ignore my letters, you turn up in Dublin – and presumably London en route – and sick to boot by the looks of you, and I'm the last person to know, I'll say I'm angry. By the way, this is my third attempt to see you today, that Valkyrie needs putting down. Here, let me look at you …

He switches on a couple of lamps, she holds up a shielding hand, he sits to take her in, blinks, shocked at the drawn white face, the empty eyes, the dead gesture of her body in the chair.

WILLIE: What is it, love? *(He sees the tears massing)* What is it? Can you say?

The tears brim over, scald her nose and cheeks. She rubs a stiff palm at them. He kneels forward, takes her hands in his to calm her, hands her his perfect apricot kerchief.

MAUD: *(Trying to gather)* Look at this *(the kerchief)* … look at you, my, you look something.

WILLIE: A chance encounter with Oscar Wilde, a couple of succès d'estime, *e presto* …

MAUD: Oh God it's so good to see you, Willie. *(Tears again, she goes to wipe them back, he stops her)* See, this is what happens, I can't stop.

WILLIE: They will out. Let them be. Mmm?

He calms her again, stands, checks out the medicines on the side-table, studies several bottles of chloroform, looks back at the pallor on her skin.

WILLIE: Is it an illness?

MAUD: Bit of bronchitis, nothing. *(Sees the bottle in his hand)* No, that's to help me sleep, just now I don't, as a rule. I've used it since … for years. It's not in the body, it's in here *(She lays a hand on her breast)*, in here *(She touches a temple)*. It's just, I can't say … I'm losing touch with my life. So many things. And every one of them hurts.

Tears again. He watches, moves back to his chair.

WILLIE: So what is it? Is it politics? Is it ..?

MAUD: Politics? Some of it, yes. I've been away too long, I don't belong any more, I'm treated like a freak and an outsider looking to butter my own loaf. I offered to raise money in America for the Wolfe Tone Centenary, the London Committee turned me down … For the first time in my life I don't know what I'm doing. I'm not sure I want to go on with politics.

Long silence. She twists the kerchief in her hands. Mrs Old arrives with the roses, lays them on a table.

MRS OLD: *(Leaving)* Ye've a hard mouth for a poet, Mister, so ye have.

Willie ignores her. Maud crosses to smell them.

MAUD: God look at them, they're beautiful.

WILLIE: Going to America, Maud, would it help?

MAUD: I don't know. It wouldn't hurt to know somebody trusted me …

WILLIE: I'll ask the Dublin Committee, will I?

MAUD: Why would they be any different?

WILLIE: I've just been elected President.

MAUD: Are you tickling me? *(He shakes his head)* That's wonderful, I had no idea.

WILLIE: There's more, isn't there? Come on, let it out. I'm staying here until I know it all.

MAUD: Why are you so good to me, Willie?

WILLIE: *(Simple)* Because I love you, Maud. And because you're Maud and I'm Willie. And if you're not you I can't be me.

Tears again; scalders. He draws her from her chair, brings her to him, holds and comforts her.

WILLIE: You know I would marry you tomorrow if you would have me. *(She spills over again, sobbing, moaning, beating the chair with her fists)* What? What have I said?

MAUD: *(Maddened by it)* You don't know anything about me, what do you imagine France has been about, do you think it was just politics ..? I've had a lover there. Since before I met you. I bore a son who died. I have a three year old daughter in a convent. And I can own to **none** of it and it's burning holes in me, Oh God Oh God Oh God, you'll hate me now and so you should, say you won't, say you won't …

The two hang close to each other in the darkening room. The roses burn on the table. Willie's face gleams over her shoulder, a lost boy.

WILLIE: I could never hate you. But can all of this be true ..? I mean.

MAUD: I cannot marry you, Willie. There is no wife in me for anyone and I have lost all feeling for the … physical, do you understand?

WILLIE: I don't love you for your sex, Maud. I love you for your spirit.

MAUD: Then we are married already, my love. A true spiritual union. *(She moves her head to look at him, their faces close)* Willie, I dreamt you last night.

WILLIE: I know.

MAUD: You came to me while I slept.

WILLIE: Yes.

MAUD: And.

He slowly places his lips on hers, like a man leaving a love-letter for an absent sweetheart.

WILLIE: *(Eventually)* Kissed you on the lips. *(Looks hard into her eyes)* Maud, come to the West with me, until you're Maud again, Maud Gonne again, there's a sacred place there I want you to see and feel, Roscommon, a lake, an island castle, will you ..?

MAUD: God, but you're a good man, Willie Yeats. See. See. I'm not crying.

He brushes hair from her eyes. Sound slowly fades. The room slowly darkens, like a stage set.

Music fades in, a piped version of The Wearing of the Green, trailing coming scene.

WILLIE: *(Over, from trance) No no, there was more, there was much more ...*

MAUD: *(Over, from trance) I don't see it, Willie. I'm Maud again.*

WILLIE: *(Over, from trance) And gone again.*

Smash cut to

INT NIGHT. OPERA HOUSE, NEW YORK. 1897

Applause, cheering, whistling, stamping.

Maud (31) stands alone before a microphone on the vast stage, staring out at the packed 2000-seat house. She wears a beautiful shimmering emerald green evening dress, holds a single half-sheet of notes in her hand. Above her, a grand banner proclaims **The Wolfe Tone Centenary Fundraising Tour/for the Freeing of Ireland/ and the Release of all Political Prisoners.**

The huge applause finally ends.

MAUD: Friends, compatriots, I thank you for the warmth of your welcome. Much praise has been bestowed on me by previous speakers, but I would have you know I stand before you as a woman of no importance who is simply performing the duty every Irishwoman owes her country. A country of plenty, where in the last hundred years one million of our people have died of starvation and a further three million have been forced to flee her shores. This year that hideous mockery the Queen's Jubilee will be celebrated, by those who care nothing for the famine and misery she has caused. Next year Ireland will celebrate her own Jubilee. *(A wave at the banner)* and your generosity will help us show the world that Ireland is united once again and will be free ...

Applause, giving way to music again, moving through

Mute montage of collections America-wide; money hits buckets, hats, collection-plates; then on to Ireland, Scotland, England, with Willie and Maud sharing platforms; arriving finally at

EXT. CHARLEMONT ST. TENEMENTS, DUBLIN. 1897. DAY.

Maud and Dagda pick their way through the rotting pavement life of the classic slum. She checks a number, climbs stone steps to an open communal front door and up again to the top of the building. Knocks at a peeling door. Studies the poster for the Irish Socialist Republican Party in the window while she waits. Six-year-old Nora Connolly answers. Stares at the giant hound, the godlike woman.

MAUD: I seek Mr Connolly, if you please, child.

A short stocky Scots Irishman around thirty appears, buttoning his shirt.

MAUD: James Connolly?

CONNOLLY: Who wants him?

MAUD: Maud Gonne. *(He sniffs. Nods.)* I hear you have plans for the Jubilee.

CONNOLLY: We do.

MAUD: I have a few of my own. Will we talk?

CONNOLLY: *(A brilliant smile)* That we will.

He lifts Nora into his arms to clear the way. Sound fades.

Maud walks in to the two-room hovel. Takes in for the first time the appalling squalor in which these lives are led. Mrs. Connolly washes two infants in a tin bath; four kids in all; she's 25 maybe. Crucifixes, sacred hearts, blessed virgin maries, palm sunday palms adorn the damp crumbling walls. Connolly and Maud sit at table to talk. The kids fuss Dagda, who's trying to eat the bath soap.

MAUD: *(Over, from trance)* It was you said I should go, I wouldn't have bothered. But such a day will change a life …

Moving to

Mute montage of images of Municipal Preparations for the official Jubilee Celebrations across Dublin, intercut with images of Nationalist anti-Jubilee preparations to sabotage it, including

*Maud and Willie making black flags for the demonstrations; Maud and Connolly selecting images from Maud's personal collection of land eviction slides for use on the big day; committee on committee, all of them, arguing the toss; working on a coffin and a banner to drape it reading: **The British Empire R.I.P.**; Connolly briefing electricity workers around a map of the city on the timing of the required power-cut; writing and printing handbills with Arthur Griffith at the offices of **The United Irishman**; Maud and Willie giving secret briefings to the world's press; women's groups, workers' groups, middle-class sponsors and patrons groups …*

WILLIE: *(Over, from trance)* Such a time, such a time. Was it ever better than this, Maud?

MAUD: *(Over, from trance)* Everything seemed possible. What could be better, Willie? And it marked us all. Our 'terrible beauty' I think you called it, later on. Of which, in this time anyway, you were wholly a part …

Mute montaged images of the anti-Jubilee actions:

The vice-regal procession, ceremonial coaches draped with union flags and flanked by military outriders, turns into O'Connell Street. Crowds line the pavements, sullen, silent. At a signal from anti-Jubilee marshalls, segments of the crowd hoist their black flags. Police rush in to quell the movement, fights break out as the crowd struggles to keep them out. Moving to

Parnell Square, evening, light fading. Furtive street-lit preparations underway for an open-air anti-Jubilee meeting, Maud vividly in view. Men fit a projection screen to a large upper window of the National Club, Maud mounts a makeshift platform to survey the space. A crowd begins to form as if by magic from the sidestreets and passageways. Maud checks her watch. Moving to

Generator Plant: Connolly's electrical workers check their watches, a silent countdown. A bulb-lit map of the city shows lights on everywhere. At a signal, several handswitches are plunged, the map bulbs for the Parnell Square area go out.

Parnell Square plunges into darkness, the swelling crowd roaring its approval. An eviction slide suddenly appears on the Club window-screen. Lamps appear in the crowd; organisers move forward to light the platform and Maud. Applause.

MAUD: *(full sound suddenly)* … Today, my friends, we are invited to celebrate the Famine Queen's 60th year in office. We thought it right that we should review what she has done for Ireland … *(Slide by slide piles up the casual horror)* … Donegal, Mayo, Roscommon, Galway, Sligo, Limerick … A proud record of achievement to take with her to her royal grave.

Squads of police arrive in the Square, whistles blowing; loudspeakers blare out their warnings, Connolly's men and Maud's women form a human cordon around the listeners, fights break out, Maud's women refuse to budge and have to be carried away. Anti-Jubilee marshalls move in to ferry the crowd away to Dame Street. Maud leaps into a car driven by Willie and away. She shrieks with laughter. Willie drives like a madman through the moil.

Mute images of Dame Street demo: Connolly leads a torchlit procession towards College Green, the coffin and British Empire R.I.P. banner at its head on a rickety handwagon. The procession swells as the Parnell Square crowd begin to filter in. Maud and Willie arrive, join Connolly and Griffith in the van, under I.R.S.P and United Irishman banners. Byestanders applaud, some join.

Police on horseback appear from sidestreets up ahead. The March heads straight through them, the police regroup, draw batons, charge into the March. Fights, shrieks, men and horses down, panic.

The leading group rush the bier-wagon towards the Liffey, horsemen give chase. At the bridge, Connolly lifts the coffin from the wagon and hurls it into the river. A great cheer goes up from crowd and onlookers. Maud's face, exultant; Willie's, demonic. They share a grin. The horsemen charge into them, batons flailing. Paddywagons rush up, arrestees are dragged and thrown into them. Connolly goes down, blood flowing from a scalp wound. People begin to scatter.

Full sound abruptly in. Willie grabs Maud's arm, draws her after him into a maze of dockside ginnels, alleys, snicks, freeze in doorways as marauding mounted police search the area. Arrive eventually at a stairway to a basement apartment, go down to hide among the dustbins in the tiny front yard. They gasp for breathe, exhilarated, scared, alive to everything.

WILLIE: By God we showed 'em, Maud, we showed 'em.

MAUD: *(Gasping)* I feel such a coward running away.

WILLIE: You'll get over it. In any case, who's going to help bail the folk arrested if we're all inside?

MAUD: You're so calm, Willie. Look at you.

WILLIE: Once I'd decided I was going to have my skull broken, I stopped worrying …

Sounds of horsemen approaching up above, calls, shouts, a demonstrator sprints by, the hooves quicken to follow. Maud and Willie paste themselves to the wall between the overflowing dustbins. The sounds leak away down the street. They find themselves sitting in the spilled rubbish: rags, bones, assorted trash. Willie picks around in it, fascinated.

MAUD: What are you doing?

WILLIE: I'm rooting. People's lives. *(He's piecing the torn photograph of a young woman together)* People's hearts.

He roots on. Handles an animal bone; a raggedy cotton stocking. She watches him. He looks up at her.

MAUD: There are times I love you so much, Willie.

WILLIE: Marry me, Maud. *(She shakes her head)* Live with me.

MAUD: You're part of me, Willie. I'm part of you. You need to be a poet. I need to be a free woman.

WILLIE: Can I meet your daughter?

MAUD: Of course. Iseult.

WILLIE: Iseult. Mm. Remember the play I said I'd write you? *(She nods, eyes bright)* It's almost done.

MAUD: I want to be the first to read it.

WILLIE: You will be. *(Shouts in the street above, close for a moment, fading, gone)* … I don't want to lose you, Maud, you know? You marry someone else, suddenly we're … nothing …

MAUD: *(Approaching, holding him to her)* Never. Never never never. Never.

Long overhead shot of the huddled pair among the debris.

Sound fades.

WILLIE: *(Over , from trance)* All the nevers in the world. And yet, and yet …

The image slowly reverts back to seascreen.

WILLIE: *(Over, from trance)* Maud?

MAUD: *(Over, from trance)* Nothing there. Blank. (Long pause) Wait!

The seascreen flickers into image, becomes

EXT. DAY. PLATFORM, GARE DE LYON, PARIS. 1901.

Mute images of Maud (35) waiting to meet someone from the train. She carries a small placard with L' IRLANDE LIBRE on it. Behind her, a small group of women carry a banner of welcome reading **The Daughters of Erin, Paris Section, welcome Major John MacBride, Commander of the Transvaal Irish Brigade and Hero of the War against the British in South Africa.**

Maud's watching face, focusing on someone some distance down the platform.

On the reverse we see

John MacBride, mid-thirties, in the uniform of a Major in the Irish Brigade, striding powerfully towards her through the throng, his pack over his shoulder. He's a sinewy, seeming-gentle Mayo man, heavily moustached, burnt by the sun.

Maud's face, taking him in.

Her point of view. The unstoppable advance continues.

WILLIE: *(Over, from trance) Never never never never never.*

The image of the striding soldier slows, breaks up, degrades back into seascreen.

VISION ENDS

Shot of the sea, immediately pre-dawn.

Reverse to show the house perched on Howth Head. The attic windows burn yellow against the lightening sky, Magritte-like.

Cut to

INT. ATTIC.

Maud sleeps on her chaise, Willie watches her from his chair.

The Bailey light suddenly cuts. The Burmese gong sets up its humming. The water in the bowl is all but still.

Fade to black.

Fade up

EXT. GARDEN. EARLY AFTERNOON.

Willie sits at a parasolled table reading a paper amid the debris of breakfast.

Maud's manuscript lies open on the table beneath the newspaper.

INT. STAIRS.

Maud arriving in the hall, headed for the garden. Jane sees her from the kitchen, calls her softly, beckons her for a confidential word, a slip of paper in her hand.

JANE: Mr Sweeney took a call for you this morning, mum. No message. Just left his name.

MAUD: *(Taking the note)* Thank you, Jane. Is Mr Sweeney about?

JANE: *(Leaving)* He's fetching Rooney's boat, mum. I'll bring the tea.

Maud frowns: Rooney's boat? She studies the note. It bears the one word, in Sweeney's unschooled hand: **finergun.**

EXT. GARDEN.

Willie turns to take her in as she crosses the lawn, stands to back a chair for her.

WILLIE: I trust you slept well, we have a busy day ahead.

MAUD: Well, as long as it involves nothing more strenuous than a gentle ramble in the orchard and a game of croquet. Ah. Soda bread.

She lays some on her plate, finds the butter. Jane appears with a fresh pot of tea, pours, leaves. Willie's returned to his paper.

WILLIE: It seems there's not to be a war after all. The English and the Germans have decided to hold a peace conference. *(Laughs)* That's like having a pair of necrophiliacs run a mortuary.

MAUD: Willie, please, I'm trying to eat.

WILLIE: We made a good start, Maud.

MAUD: And did you find what you were after?

WILLIE: No, but I will before we finish, I know it.

MAUD: I thought we <u>had</u> finished.

WILLIE: How do you mean?

MAUD: The book, Willie. We reached the last page of my memoir, nineteen three or whenever it was. Wasn't that the journey?

WILLIE: *(Laying paper down)* There's more, Maud. We can't leave it there.

MAUD: Why not? It's where I left the book.

WILLIE: But not the life. I need it all.

Silence. She sips her tea. Looks out across the heat-hazed sound.

MAUD: Willie, my book stops there because I cannot deal with the rest. It's too painful. Too raw.

WILLIE: Try, love. I beg you.

Silence. Their eyes lock; their wills.

Sweeney appears at the bottom of the garden.

SWEENEY: *(Calling)* Ready when you are, milord.

WILLIE: *(Cool)* With you in a moment.

SWEENEY: Rooney wants it back by five at the latest …

WILLIE: *(Iced)* Thank you, Mr Sweeney.

Sweeney evaporates. His wife appears from the house, Maud's cloak in her hands; lays it on a chairback. Maud stares at it, frowns. Willie gathers a leather bag by his chair, puts on his coat.

WILLIE: All set?

MAUD: For what? Where are we going?

Fade in

Rasp of outboard motor at full-throttle, cut to

EXT. SEA.

Tight shot of prow of small boat powering through waves.

The shot tilts up to take in Ireland's Eye looming from the water two hundred yards ahead.

Sweeney steers at the rear; Willie and Maud are up front, staring at the island. Behind them, the mainland, Howth Head just visible in the haze, a mile away.

EXT. SHINGLE COVE, IRELAND'S EYE.

The boat's been beached on shingles, Sweeney carries Willie's bag up to the mouth of a cave a few feet above sea-level. Willie watches him from a ledge.

Maud stands aloof, not wholly pleased, in the entrance to the cave, gazing in.

SWEENEY: *(Plonking bag down)* I'll catch some fish. Half four suit ye?

WILLIE: *(Checking watch)* Stay close, the weather may turn around.

Sweeney makes a long deliberate scan of the unblemished sky. Locates a solitary scrawl of white cloud in the vast blue.

SWEENEY: Ah. Look at that devil there, could be the tip o' the ice cube, right enough.

He heads back for the boat. Willie begins unloading the bag and laying things out in the mouth of the cave: firewood, charcoal, matches; a metal cup, a small dagger, a disc, a wand, a sword, a lotus wand, a Rose cross with a fixing pin. Maud has turned to watch him. He pours paraffin over the firewood and charcoal cobs; lays out two cushions. Looks up at her.

MAUD: No bowler hat and butcher's apron, no rolled trouser-leg ..?

WILLIE: *(Patting a cushion)* Come.

She wanders over, joins him by the readying fire.

MAUD: Only for you, Willie. And don't blame me if it comes out wrong, I'm really not ready for this …

He pins the Rose cross to her breast.

WILLIE: *(Naming them in turn)* Love *(the rose)*, water *(the cup)*, air *(the dagger)*, earth *(the disc)*, invocations *(the lotus wand)*, energy *(the sword)* … *(He lays the wand across the charcoal, strikes a match, holds it above the pile)* Fire.

The match falls, the pile lights, paraffin first, wood, wand, charcoal. He picks up the lotus wand, begins a Kabalic invocation, his eyes burning into the blaze.

Maud watches him a moment, resisting; eventually turns her eyes to the flame.

Willie sets up his weird chanting throatsong: **Cathleen's Song**.

WILLIE: They shall be remembered forever
                They shall be alive for ever
                They shall be speaking for ever
                The people shall hear them for ever

Close shot of the blaze, sound gradually fading, image slowing to flamescreen.

SECOND VISION

A single red-gel spot emerges, kicks suddenly to life. Cut to

INT. ST THERESA'S TOTAL ABSTINENCE HALL, DUBLIN. 1902.

The front of house spot hits a stooped old woman front of stage. She gazes blindly into it at the packed, expectant house. Straightens to a full majestic six feet, the cloak sliding to the boards, revealing the brilliant green of the dress beneath. The shot closes on her as she begins to speak.

MAUD/CATHLEEN: It is a hard service they take who help me. Many that are red-cheeked now will be pale-cheeked; many that have been free to walk the hills and the bogs and the rushes will be sent to walk hard streets in far countries; many a good plan will be broken; many that have gathered money will not stay to spend it; many a child will be born and there will be no father at its christening to give it a name. They that have red cheeks will have pale cheeks for my sake; and for all that they will think they are well paid …

Silence. The blind eyes stare on into the dark. The audience sets up a chant: Cathleen Cathleen Cathleen ….

Sound fades.

Trail MacBride's voice, a hopeless cry: She has maligned me, she has dishonoured me, she has unmanned me …gavelling throughout. Cut to

INT. CIVIL COURTROOM, PARIS. 1906.

John MacBride, wrecked, desperate, struggles with his lawyers and court ushers trying to push him back into his chair. The Judge gavels for silence.

MACBRIDE: *(As he's overpowered)* … I want my son, let her go to hell but let me, I beg you, let me have my son …

He weeps, reduced. The judge waits quietly for calm; glances at Maud (40), who sits upright, aloof, beside her lawyer; at the children, Iseult (12), Seán (2), on his nurse's knee, in the well beyond her. Takes an all's well nod from MacBride's lawyer. Resumes his written judgment.

JUDGE: *(In French; a lawyer feeds MacBride translation)* … In addition to the aforementioned weekly right of visitation, the father shall have the right to sole custody for the month of August until the son shall attain the age of 16 years …

Maud's eyes close in shock and horror, MacBride's open on hope. Maud's up on her feet at once, protesting vehemently, her lawyers struggling to calm her.

Sound fades. The packed international press gallery scribbles furiously.

MAUD: *(Over, from trance)* … One day of sole custody was all MacBride would have needed to spirit my son away to Ireland, where no court would uphold the claim of an errant wife. So any thought of raising the boy there had thus to be abandoned …

EXT. DAY. LES MOUETTES, NORMANDY COAST. SOME MONTHS LATER.

A voiture - a large farm cart with hooped canvas covering – drives Maud, Iseult, Seán, maid and menagerie to her summer house by the sea.

MAUD: *(Over, from trance)* … And the long years of virtual exile had begun …

Maud looks ahead towards the house. Sees a solitary figure waiting amid his luggage by the gate.

Maud's face, trying to make the figure out, blinking with joy when she realises who it is.

ISEULT: Who is it, Maman?

MAUD: It's Uncle Willie.

SEAN: Willie willie willie …

Long shot of the carriage's arrival, greetings, introductions, the slow ragged drift inside.

INT. MID-EVENING, SOME HOURS LATER. LARGE COUNTRY KITCHEN.

Maud writes letters by candlelight amid the debris of dinner, which the maid is trying to clear. Mounds of box-files litter the work-surface: Irlande Libre, Daughters of Erin, Clann naGael, Irish Socialist Workers Party, Irish National Theatre Board, Irish Party, Prisoners Defence League, School Dinners …

From upstairs, the sounds of Willie reading bedtime stories and poems to the children, amid gasps, whoops and laughter. Maud frowns smilingly at the din, lays down her pen, walks to the bottom of the stairs.

MAUD: *(Calling)* Willie, in case you've forgotten, the object of the exercise is to get the little pests to sleep … *(The children shout their protests, Willie hushes them.)* Any more of your cheek, Miss Gonne, and you'll spend tomorrow working the vegetable patch instead of seeing Mont St Michel.

She smiles her way back to her work. Lights a cigarette. The maid removes the last of the crockery to the scullery.

Willie in, pale suit, brown face, eyes gleaming. Joins Maud across the table.

MAUD: What do you think?

WILLIE: *(Headshake)* Couple of brats, no question. I adore them.

MAUD: They like you. *(Willie pours them more wine)* I have never known a man more generous, more loving, more everything than you. I'm so happy you came. So happy you're here.

WILLIE: *(Glass raised)* To families.

They clink, drink; she smiles, he stares at her shimmering face in the candlelight. Silence.

WILLIE: What are you working on?

MAUD: *(A wave across the files)* Oh, everything. Just now I'm focusing on children. Did you know the British Provision of School Dinners Act specifically excludes Ireland? *(He shakes his head)* How can that be justified? How?

WILLIE: It can't. *(He takes in the files; the labour)* You are. Quite unstoppable. Mrs …

He cuts, not comfortable with the rest. The Maid appears from the scullery, en route for bed.

MAID: Bonne nuit, Madame. Je m'en vais.

MAUD: *(Crossing to hug her)* Bonne nuit, Charlotte. Et merci. Demain tu seras libre, ça va? Prends quoi que tu veux de l'armoire … Oui oui.

She leaves. Maud returns to her wine, lights another cigarette.

WILLIE: You know, for a woman who's been dragged through hell by the heels, you look a treat. Was it awful?

MAUD: Not all of it. I have a son again. Iseult came through unscathed. There's much to be thankful for.

WILLIE: I have <u>read</u> the public prints, Maud. It wasn't all good news.

MAUD: No. It wasn't all good news. I fell to a brave revolutionary hero, but I married a deeply conventional little man. There we are.

WILLIE: Five nevers, Maud. Five. I really imagined you meant never.

MAUD: I did. And I paid for it. And I'm sorry. Don't ask me.

WILLIE: What a swine.

MAUD: No.

WILLIE: Drunken fits, brutal assaults, animal demands ..? **No?**

MAUD: It's how men are, Willie. If we want to change it, we have to change how they're raised. Pour me some wine.

He pours more red. She strokes his pouring hand with a finger.

MAUD: How long do you have?

WILLIE: In France? Couple of weeks. I'm meeting people in Paris but.

MAUD: Are they important? *(He shrugs)* I know I haven't the right to ask, but I'd love you to stay.

WILLIE: You have the right.

MAUD: Then will you?

WILLIE: *(After thought)* I might.

She blinks. He grins. Sound fades. She throws her head back, laughs.

Her long gleaming hair rears in slowed motion, live, writhing. His eyes glisten, living her.

MAUD: *(Over, from trance)* The last of the beautiful days, Willie.

MAINLY MUTE MONTAGE. THAT SUMMER. NORMANDY.

Deserted beach. Willie and Seán fly a painted Chinese hawk kite high above the tide flats. Maud and Iseult sit with a hamper and books in the dunes, watching them.

MONT ST MICHEL. They wander en famille around the ancient walls and yards of the sacred redoubt. Willie secures Seán by the legs on the highest wall to look out at the sea.

TIDE FLATS. Maud and Seán gather seashells and pebbles in a box. Return to the dunes, where Willie recites poetry to Iseult, whose head rests on his shoulder.

SEA. They swim naked, all four of them, in the lee of high limestone rocks. The dogs stand in the shallows barking, scared to go in.

VOITURE, heading back to the summerhouse. The four sit in silence, as if acknowledging the end of something. The sinking sun washes their faces.

Full sound resumes as we move to

INT. LES MOUETTES, KITCHEN. NIGHT.

Willie sits by the big black stove, stowing books and notebooks in a bag and listening to Maud upstairs comforting an inconsolable Sean. A mantel clock ticks determinedly in the still room.

Iseult appears in the doorway in her nightdress, finger to lips. Willie looks a question at her.

ISEULT: This is for you, Willie.

He takes the painting, studies it. A man and a woman stand hand in hand before the summer house looking out at the viewer. A young girl with long flaxen hair and a squit of a boy, badly drawn, play on the edges of the scene. She's called it 'Willie and Maud' in bold script.

WILLIE: Thank you.

He opens his arms, she melts into the hug, he kisses her head and hair.

ISEULT: Just so you don't forget us.

He shakes his head, moved. She bobs forward to kiss his cheek. Tiptoes away.

Willie stares at the picture a moment. Frowns. Looks more closely. On the reverse, we see a small green aura around the man's head and upper body. He looks after her to the doorway. Sees Maud there, grave-eyed, just arrived, watching him.

WILLIE: What?

MAUD: Nothing.

She crosses to pour herself a drink and stand by the window. Stares out at the bruised sky.

MAUD: He's inconsolable, the boy. Says we won't ever see you again.

WILLIE: Fat chance.

He closes the bag, takes it through to the next room, comes back with another one, begins stashing shoes, boots, leggings laid out in the hearth.

MAUD: I may be in Ireland in the Autumn. A week or two. Lady Gregory has sent me a ticket to her première. It'll be a great Irish occasion, I think I should be there.

WILLIE: Are you sure?

MAUD: What do you mean?

WILLIE: It hasn't occured to you, has it? You're a National Scandal, Maud. The Catholic Heart of Ireland has been seriously attacked by your conduct, people can't wait to get you in their sights, they will make your public life unbearable …

MAUD: No they won't. They don't have the power to do that.

WILLIE: Fine. Then we'll walk in together, arm in arm.

MAUD: *(She smiles, loving him)* Done.

She joins him by the stove. Watches him packing. He stops, sits back, looks across at her. The clock ticks stolidly on.

WILLIE: This is the longest we've ever spent. All the years.

MAUD: I know.

WILLIE: Hasn't been bad, has it?

MAUD: I have loved this time, Willie.

WILLIE: Beautiful days. They've given me something very dear. A place in your family. A place in your heart. Uncle Willie. But if I'm to be truthful … *(He closes the bag, carries it to the next room. Maud takes out her cigarettes, puts one to her mouth, fumbles for her matches. He returns, lights a taper at the stove, holds it to her face)* … I'm actually rather glad to be leaving.

They look at each other close up across the flame. She dips for the light, comes up smoking. He keeps the taper up, as if to light her or fend her off.

MAUD: Glad?

WILLIE: Yes. Maybe relieved's the word I want.

MAUD: Relieved. What like a fortress, like an occupied city ..?

WILLIE: No, like a man, Maud.

MAUD: Like a man.

WILLIE: Indeed, if I'm to be truthful …

MAUD: … Do …

WILLIE: … I'm glad or relieved to be leaving like a man who has spent the last four weeks enjoying every possible intimacy with the woman he loves save the one he most and most persistently desires to bursting point, namely her sexuality. In that sense, and in that sense only, it would be true to say I am relieved to be leaving. Man cannot live by hand alone, Maud. Leviticus. Forgive the candour, I don't intend to make a habit of it …

MAUD: Oscar Wilde, actually.

WILLIE: Really? *(She nods)* I needed to raise this, love. It's not easy. And I'm quite bitter, underneath. So.

Remote sound of train hooting the night.

MAUD: What about that hashish you spoke of in Paris? Do you have some?

WILLIE: Ahunh. Want to try?

MAUD: Mmm.

He carries a lamp into the other room, searches for the gear in a bag. She follows. He lays the stuff out on his makeshift bed, sits to get it together: wooden pipe, resin, tobacco.

Maud moves in, hovers in the half-light.

WILLIE: To frustrate that which you excite would in some seem serious cruelty. But you have the singleminded innocence of the uncorrupted child, my love, and give it no thought …

MAUD: Do you have other women ..?

WILLIE: I do.

MAUD: And do they ..?

WILLIE: They do.

MAUD: Oh. And is it ..?

WILLIE: It is. More or less.

MAUD: Who, for instance?

WILLIE: Florence.

MAUD: Florence Farr? *(He nods)* She's a fine woman.

WILLIE: Indeed. Mabel Beardsley?

MAUD: The …

WILLIE: … Physiotherapist, yes.

MAUD: Mmm.

He lights the pipe, inhales, holds, releases. Hands it to Maud.

WILLIE: Just one. It's enough.

She takes the hit. Waits. Lets it out. Blinks.

WILLIE: We could still get married.

MAUD: I am married.

WILLIE: I can wait. The court's offered you a divorce in two years.

MAUD: I didn't ask and I won't file. In any case …

WILLIE: *(Waiting)* …What?

MAUD: What?

WILLIE: In any case **what**?

MAUD: I don't know what you want. This marriage, this hot sticky gruel of relationship. There is a mother in me, there is a sister in me, there is a daughter in me, there is no wife in me, Willie, not for you, not for any man, especially not for you, I'm the last person on earth you should seek to marry, posterity will surely thank me for my consistent 'No', no poet should ever marry … Are we arguing?

WILLIE: Arguing? Who?

They chuckle. She moves in to the bedspace, sits back to the wall on the floor to face him.

MAUD: When I come over.

WILLIE: Autumn.

MAUD: I want to see the Castle.

WILLIE: Lough Key.

MAUD: Show me.

WILLIE: The mysteries.

MAUD: Yes.

The mantel clock whirs and strikes: eleven.

Sudden flash images of gold and blue medieval oars on stretch of lake intersperse:

WILLIE: And the oars that take us to that holy place
                      Across that sacred lough shall be of no
                      Ordinary wood, your beech, your cherry, but
                      Sandal from the East gilded blade to fist
                      And tipped in Ravenna's brightest blue …

WILLIE: *(Over, from trance, stirred by oars on water)* Ha. There again, close, close.

The vision steadies, wholly restoring to the Les Mouettes present. They stare at each other across the room; magically stoned.

Moving to

INTERIORS. MAUD'S BEDROOM/ WILLIE'S. THROUGH THE NIGHT.

Mute shot of Maud lying naked on her bed, unmoving as if asleep, eyes open.

Mute shot of Willie, naked on his bed, eyes closed as if in sleep.

Maud sits up suddenly, eyes open. Listens.

Willie's face, barely lit in the darkened room. Sounds of someone close by, closing. His eyes open. See

Maud – or someone like her, or an outline of her – standing by the bed. He holds his arms out, she moves to him, folds herself to him on the bed.

WILLIE: *(Over, from trance)* The dreams were real, Maud.

MAUD: *(Over, from trance)* Real Dreams.

SOUND sifts slowly through into the shot. Breathing, moaning, tiny mutters, the slide of flesh on flesh in the darkened room.

Other sounds, perhaps distant thunder, or premonitory cannonades from the coming war …

They love on, oblivious.

Moving to

Mute bleached shot of oars in rainpocked water, dipping and lifting.

WILLIE: *(Over, from trance)* Yes yes yes, there was more, I knew it.

The shot tilts up to reveal a rowing boat on the Seine (1912), caught in a downpour. Willie (47) pulls hard for the bank, urged on by Iseult(18) and Seán (8). Maud (46) waits for them under a stand of elms on the bank.

WILLIE: *(Over, from trance)* No no no, where is it, where is it ..?

Moving abruptly to

INT. SANATORIUM. LOURDES. 1914.

MAUD lies propped in a darkened room, writing a letter. A nursing nun works round her, taking temperature and pulse and entering readings on a chart.

MAUD: *(Letter voice over)* … The Home Rule Act must not be allowed to stand, we have been betrayed again, and blood will flow until the six northern counties are returned where they belong. The papers tell me Ireland sits on the brink of civil war, Ulster Volunteers armed to the teeth by Germans at one end and Irish Volunteers armed to the teeth by Germans at the other, and I must do what I can to get home to do my share as soon as I'm well enough to travel. I am waiting for the paper with breathless anxiety and can hardly sleep for thinking of it all … How are you, where are you and why don't you write to me? We missed you so much this summer, I explained you had to visit America but the children were desolated at not having their Uncle Willie visit, and your absence left me feeling unwanted and for the first time rather old … I had a haunting sort of vision the other night, Willie, which troubles me a lot: death and famine everywhere and my dear Dublin in flames …

A doctor enters, smiles, checks the Nurse's readings, listens to Maud's lungs, front and back.

DOCTOR: *(In French)* Another week, maybe two, and you'll be well enough to get back to your beloved Ireland, Madame.

MAUD: Thank the lord.

DOCTOR: *(laying a folded copy of Le Figaro on her bed)* Provided you can get passage that is …

He leaves with the nurse. Maud frowns, stretches for the paper, opens it. It carries a single headline in huge letters: La Guerre.

She closes her eyes. Opens them. Tears grease her cheeks.

Moving to

INT. TROOP HOSPITAL, PYRENEES/ TROOP HOSPITAL, PARIS.

Brief mute sequence of images of Maud (pushing 50) and Iseult (20 or so) nursing the tidal waves of wounded Frenchmen home from the front. Seán (early teens) works as a runner and general help.

MAUD: *(Over, from trance)* Look, look at it, these men who run this world, look what they have given us, and go on giving us.

Cut to

INT. HOSPITAL, PARIS. DAY. 1916.

Maud moves at speed down corridor writhing with trainloads of young wounded just arriving. A second nurse keeps pace with her, pointing the way.

Cut to

INT. CRAMPED LINEN ROOM.

A young, corn-haired nurse stares out of the solitary window, her back to the shot. On the window sill by her hand, a jug of water and a bottle of belladonna.

The door swings open behind her, she turns to look: Iseult.

Maud stands in the doorway, strong but scared. Studies her daughter's face, ravaged by agonies of grief and despair.

Maud takes her in her arms to soothe her. Looks down at the bottle on the window sill. Sound suddenly in: trail the dull bump of great guns opening up at distance. Cut to

EXT. LATE MAY. DAY. HEADLAND OVER NORMANDY COAST. 1916

Maud stands in dune grass, listening to the war twenty miles upcoast. The great guns bump calmly away, on and on: unreal.

In closer shot, the face is worn, the eyes losing belief, a touch hopeless.

A bicycle bell draws her gaze to the house. The postman waves to her, on his way again.

INT. HOUSE. HALLWAY.

She stands in the hallway staring at the copy of The Times she's just opened. Her face maps her emotions, powerful, contradictory, alive.

INT. BACKDOORWAY.

Through open door, we see Seán working the vegetable patch. Maud calls him, out of shot. He saunters up, alert, self-confident.

MAUD: Seán. Your father has died a hero's death in a great rising in Ireland. I believe you can be proud this day, Bichon.

SEÁN: Right. *(Thinks)* How did he die?

MAUD: At the hands of a British firing squad.

She hands him the paper.

SEÁN: Right. Will I pack my things?

INT. FRONT ROOM.

Iseult sits listlessly at the window, eyes fixed on nothing. She's waxen; passive; lost in the madness of her moment.

MAUD: *(from doorway)* Iseult. *(Iseult looks across at her).* We're going home, my love.

Iseult's face slowly crumples. It takes a while to realise it's joy she's weeping for.

EXT. DAY. AT SEA.

A channel steamer's bows plough through rough fog-trapped seas.

MAUD: *(Over, from trance)* No more, Willie. I cannot deal with these days, the centre cannot hold.

The shot slows, stutters ...

WILLIE: *(Over, from trance; intense)* On. You must. We sow the seed, we reap the harvest, let the rose bleed.

Becoming

Mute bleached montage – a sort of raw footage – of the return to Ireland:

Willie awaits them at Southampton Docks. Spots them and their menagerie – 10 canaries, 1 parrot, 1 monkey, 2 cats, 1 dog – descending the gangway. He's 52, a little thicker at waist and spectacle lens, well-dressed, sage-like. He kissses Maud's cheek, then Iseult's, a grave handshake for Seán. The dock area around them fills up with British wounded, back from the war.

CUSTOM SHED. Maud and Iseult are singled out for strip-search in a back room. A court officer serves her with a Defence of the Realm Act notice banning further passage to Ireland.

Boat again. Fog again. An ancient peasant woman, weirdly reminiscent of the disguised Cathleen Ní Houlihan seen earlier, stands by the prow watching the coast of Ireland forming through the mist.

MAUD: *(Over throughout, from trance)* Half a war to get us home and once again outside the law ... God's own country, still ruled by the Devil.

MAYOR'S HALL, DUBLIN. SPRING, 1918.

Packed meeting. The platform bears leading members – men and women – of the anti-British Alliance. Behind and above them, banners and posters proclaiming affiliations (SINN FEIN prominent) and campaign issues. A strap banner the width of the stage subsumes the rest: **No Conscription for the Murder Machine - Oppose the Act.**

Audience and platform, in black armbands, stand together in a minute's silence for the Easter Dead.

Sound abruptly up as they resume seats. Arthur Griffith, in the chair, welcomes Maud Gonne MacBride back to the country and the struggle. She stands, approaches the microphone. An uncertain moment, then applause begins to spread and deepen. The platform stands too: among them, Con Markiewicz, Kathleen Clarke, Helena Maloney, Hannah Sheehy-Skeffington.

Maud's face, worn, grave, a smile growing as the applause swells.

MAUD: Friends, men and women of Ireland, I thank you. Let the message go out from this meeting tonight that Irish people across the land will resist – with their lives, if forced to – this infamous Act of Conscription in Ireland decreed by the foreign Parliament of a foreign power. And let it be understood and dutifully passed on by those in this Hall who secretly serve the British yoke, that from this day force will be met by force in this matter ... Tell your masters, for I know you are here, that Ireland demands but one Act only from the British State: the Freedom of Ireland Act.

Huge applause again. She sips from her glass. The doors at the back of the hall burst open, police and soldiers rip into the hall, declare the meeting to be seditious and place the whole gathering under arrest.

Sound fades on the mayhem of cracked heads and scuffles. Marshalls protect the platform, as the leaders make their exits, Maud among them.

INT. APARTMENT, STEPHEN'S GREEN. DAY.

Full sound. Maud and Seán unpack boxes and bags, moving in. Seán wears Fianna uniform; the youth movement of the IRA. The doorbell rings, Maud goes to answer it. Finds Willie on the step.

MAUD: Ha. You're over, you can help us move in, come in.

WILLIE: No, better not, I can't stop, I er ...

He scans the street, looking for surveillance.

MAUD: What is it, love?

WILLIE: I had dinner with the Attorney-General the other evening.

MAUD: … The <u>British</u> Attorney-General ..?

WILLIE: … There's a list being prepared, your name's on it.

MAUD: Ahunh. What do you suggest I do?

WILLIE: Leave Dublin. Lie low. Abandon all political action.

MAUD: Is that all?

WILLIE: Armed struggle is not the answer, Maud. It will get worse. Violence and terror, breeding like maggots in a boneyard. I want to help.

MAUD: Thank you.

WILLIE: *(Turning away, then back)* I'm to be married on Saturday.

MAUD: Ah.

WILLIE: Georgie Hyde Lees.

MAUD: Mm. Iseult said no then.

WILLIE: Mm. *(They look at each other)* I plan to live in Ireland.

MAUD: Good. We have room if you need it, while you find a place.

WILLIE: Thanks.

Silence. He leaves. She watches.

EXT. ROADWAY, STEPHEN'S GREEN. DAY.

Mute slowed shot through barred window, from moving vehicle, of the uniformed Seán (14) giving chase, calling and sobbing, shrinking as the van picks up speed.

MAUD: *(Over, from trance)* No no. No no no …

On the reverse, we see Maud's face at the police van window, watching her life disappear.

The shot stills to freeze. Stutters. Freezes again.

Another still frame: Maud with others, shackled on the deck of a boat. The image kicks into life briefly, freezes again.

Frame after frame, charting the way to the gates of Holloway Prison.

INT. PRE -DAWN. AUTUMN, 1918. PRISON CELL.

Full sound. Wispy light from yard lamps lightens the rough stone cell. The shot moves across the inmates' faces: Con Markiewicz, Kathleen Clarke, Hannah Sheehy-Skeffington; all sleeping; arrives finally with Maud (52), lying half-propped on her cot, coughing, delirious, half-dead.

MAUD: *(Over, from trance) Five months? Five lifetimes? The last weeks I saw death each night at dawn. Summoned to watch …*

A prison bell clock sounds the hour: seven. The light grows stronger from the coming day. She moves her feet to the stone floor, struggles to upright, moves unsteadily to the high window, lifts a stool with great effort, lays it beneath the window, begins her impossible climb.

Her head, clearing the window ledge, light striking the face. Sounds of a single drum beat, trailed from her coming vision, replace the ambient synch.

Light brightens to epiphany on her face as she scans the yard below.

We take her point of view: see

MOUNTJOY GAOLYARD, DUBLIN, SUMMER, 1916.

James Plunkett is marched to the pole at the top of the yard to the beat of the drum. Squaddies tie him to the pole; secure the blindfold. A priest prays with Plunkett for a moment, mouth to ear. An officer marches the firing squad into positions, hands out the cartridges. Aim. Fire. Puffs of smoke, Plunkett sags. The officer walks forward, pistol cocked; fires a shot into the man's head. squaddies move in to lift the body and throw it into a waiting cart filled with quicklime, as

James Connolly is carried out unconscious tied to a kitchen chair, his legs shattered by bullets. The nightmare repeats itself. As Connolly's body hits the quicklime,

John MacBride is being marched to the pole. He refuses the blindfold; dies shouting defiance.

WILLIE: *(Over,throughout, a whisper, from trance)* …
                 And what if excess of love
                 Bewildered them till they died?
                 I write it out in verse –
                 MacDonagh and MacBride
                 And Connolly and Pearse
                 Now and in time to be,
                 Wherever green is worn,
                 Are changed, changed utterly;
                 A terrible beauty is born.

Maud's watching face, in restored natural light, at the bars of her cell window. Pulmonary blood has seeped from her mouth and onto her chin. A motor horn hoots down in the yard. She looks. Sees

EXT. HOLLOWAY PRISON YARD.

An ambulance backing towards the main building from the main gate. Two warders stretcher a woman out towards the van.

Cut to

EXT. YARD.

Mute close shot of stretcher being lifted into the ambulance: it's Maud. The shot slows, stutters, stills to freeze; flames from the Ireland's Eye cave fire char and melt the still; a new image lies below it, a close shot of

Maud's face, black-veiled, red-eyed, ravaged, waiting outside

EXT. STEPHEN'S GREEN FLAT. EARLY MORNING. NOVEMBER, 1918.

Maud stands on the step amid her bags. Tries the bell again. Thin sifting drizzle mists the lamplit air.

The big oak door opens, Willie stands there in green pyjamas, straight from his bed.

WILLIE: Maud? I thought you were confined in hospital still.

MAUD: I discharged myself. Can I come in?

WILLIE: Come in? What ..?

MAUD: … I'm just in from the boat. I could use a bath and a bed.

WILLIE: I'd rather you didn't, don't you still have the room at the Nassau …?

MAUD: This is my apartment, Willie.

WILLIE: Which you have leased to me. I'm sorry. George is sick, a dreadful pneumonia, I can't risk disturbances, police raids, soldiers, she's heavy with child and … I'm sorry.

MAUD: *(Not wanting to believe this)* Willie ..?

WILLIE: It's over, Maud. It's over. I'm sorry.

MAUD: *(Sad; stony)* Oh Willie. Oh Willie. Once it was your spirit was green, now it's just your pyjamas. What a falling-off was there.

WILLIE: Let me call you a cab.

She shakes her head, gathers her bags, leaves. He stands at the door watching. She disappears into the mist.

WILLIE: *(Over, from trance) Enough.*

MAUD: *(Over, from trance) Is it?*

The image reverts to frozen flamescreen, as if over.

Jagged flashes flicker in and out, disconnected, raw footage of life beyond the moment reached. Maud's disjointed voice over from trance offers cryptic commentary.

IRA hit squads, pistols, bombs, taking out British Military Intelligence men.

MAUD: *(Over, from trance) Only for some was it enough, Willie. For others, the war never ended.*

Black and Tan terror raids: IRA youths are dragged half-dead through their home village roped to troop trucks.

Tans throw a 16-year old youth from his house into the cobbled street. Other Tans follow, the youth's mother struggling in their grip. The youth is forced to kneel; his mother is forced to watch. The Tan commander draws his pistol, holds it casually to the back of the lad's neck, fires; a simple pre-enactment of a key image from the Vietnam war.

MAUD: *(Over, from trance) And when we could no longer fight the British, we found ways to fight each other, and all of us losers, a great age had passed and genius gave way to accountancy …*

A women's prisoner's defence league banner flutters above a silent picket of twenty black-robed women outside the walls of Kilmainham gaol. Free State soldiers line the perimeter wall above them, rifles ready. Maud (almost 60) climbs onto a cart, stares up at the young Irish officer in charge. Their eyes meet; hold.

MAUD: *And. And. And …*

Full sound. In abruptly, trailing hollow metallic Prison sounds.

INT. KILMAINHAM GAOL. STONE CELL. 1923.

Mute images of Maud prostrate on her bed, half dead, on her 18th day on hunger strike. A warder makes the ritual offer of food; a doctor checks her pulse, hands her a tin cup of water. She takes a sip.

Trail sounds of soldiers, shouts, laughter. Moving to

EXT. STEPHEN'S GREEN APARTMENT. EVENING. 1923.

Maud returning home along the Green. Ahead, a small crowd of onlookers watches Free State soldiers come and go through the smashed Georgian front-door of her flat. She quickens her pace. Two soldiers guarding the action block her path. A young squaddie is pouring paraffin on the great and growing mound of documents and papers they've culled from the house and piled on the pavement. Others are still arriving with more boxes.

MAUD: *(To the paraffin pourer)* What are you doing? Who's in charge here?

POURER: *(Working on, calling inside)* There's an ould biddy out here wants to know who's in charge, sir …

MAUD: I said what are you doing, young man.

An officer appears on the step, looks her up and down.

OFFICER: This your house?

MAUD: It is.

OFFICER: Authorization.

He hands her a chit. She stares at it. The officer signals the pourer away, strikes a match, drops it on the papers, returns indoors.

Msud's face, lit by the flames, watching her life burn away.

Slow creep into the bonfire: notebooks, diaries, four decades of press cuttings, pictures, photographs, messages from comrades, her children's first scrawls and drawings, letters and their envelopes by the thousand go up in the flame.

MAUD: *(Over, from trance)* Your letters too, Willie. Every single one. All gone. Enough.

Close shot of the bonfire, reduced to a smoulder of gun-metal ash.

Becoming

Close shot of the cave fire, down to dull grey ember.

VISION ENDS

EXT. IRELAND'S EYE. LATE AFTERNOON.

They sit in their separate spaces, immobilised; appalled to silence. Tears run down Maud's cheeks; she gives no sign of knowing it.

Willie very slowly slides his hand across the limestone; covers Maud's with it.

Silence.

Growing sounds of boat returning. A shout from Sweeney below. They sit on, hand on hand, in some other place.

Cut to

EXT. BOAT.

They sit in silence as the boat whines them back. Ahead, Howth and the jetty. Sweeney's catch – three or four assorted fish – slide around in the bottom. The largest, a sea bass, slides onto Willie's foot, he kicks it away.

SWEENEY: Hold the holly there, doctor. That's your supper you're toe-endin' …

Willie gives him a cold look. Sweeney hawks, spits.

MAUD: *(Suddenly)* That'll be Sligo Duck I suppose, will it?

SWEENEY: Bang on, Your Grace. The very thing.

He laughs. She smiles.

Cut to

EXT. JETTY.

Sweeney gives Maud a hand up to the boards. Willie waves the hand away; proves unable to manage the ascent; Maud has to haul him up.

WILLIE: No no, I can manage perfectly well …

Sweeney leads them off down the jetty towards the parked car, the catch in a bucket in his hand.

SWEENEY: Ye may not know it, ma'am, but just now we're treadin' sacred ground …

WILLIE: *(Throttling it back)* For God's sake man, we're treading clapboard! Sacred ground …

MAUD: How so, Mr Sweeney?

WILLIE: Don't humour him.

SWEENEY: Twas on this very jetty the guns and rounds was landed for the Rising of 19 and 16, so it was.

WILLIE: Ignore him, he's making it up …

Sweeney grins, begins whistling.

WILLIE: We won't be needing your fish, by the way. Tonight we dine out …

Sweeney stops whistling. They've reached the car. Sweeney begins spooning them in.

MAUD: Really? Where?

WILLIE: Here in Howth. But let me surprise you with it.

SWEENEY: *(Starting her up on the handle)* If it's here in Howth it'll be Malloy's, that being the only place serves a plate in the place, and if it's Malloy's, that'll be some surprise all right.

He gets behind the wheel, crunches through to first.

WILLIE: Just drive, would you. Talk is not required.

Cut to

EXT. EVENING. HEADLAND ROAD.

The Model A Ford hurtles down the winding hill towards the town. Willie and Maud hang on grimly; Sweeney sings **Patrick was a Gentleman** *with some abandon.*

SWEENEY: Patrick was a gentleman
             Came from decent people
             He built a church in Dublin town
             And on it put a steeple.
             His father was a Gallagher
             His mother was a Grady
             His aunt was an O'Shaughnessy
             His uncle was a Brady
             The Wicklow hills are very high
             And so is the hill of Howth, sir,
             But there's a hill much higher still,
             Much higher than them both, sir …

EXT. MALLOY'S BAR, A SPATCHCOCK OF RECENTLY CONVERTED COTTAGES, HOWTH HARBOUR.

Sweeney locks the car and ushers the bedecked couple into the boisterous saloon bar. He carries a brown paper bag in with him.

INT. MALLOY'S SALOON.

Maud and Willie wait by the door while Sweeney has a word with Malloy, who's serving at the bar. Malloy approaches the couple, wiping his hand for the shake, leads them through to a private room at the back.

Sweeney's left at the bar haggling with Mrs Malloy over the contents of his bag. She offers a pair of shillings. Sweeney reluctantly accepts, well pleased.

INT. PRIVATE DINING ROOM, A HALF-FLOOR UP.

Malloy disposes of their topcoats, sees them to their seats at the solitary table, lights the table candles.

MALLOY: Excuse me, Mum, but would you be Maud Gonne ..?

MAUD: I would.

MALLOY: Bless you, Mum. Tis a grave honour ye do us, mum, and a benediction on this house. I'll send the Missus right away, sir.

He backs out of the tiny room, eyes agleam at the Great Lady.

WILLIE: You should go on the boards, ye'd clean up.

MAUD: So write me a play.

They gaze at each other through the smoky candles.

WILLIE: I would too. If there were time. *(He scans the whitewashed walls)* What do you think?

MAUD: It's … cosy.

WILLIE: You don't recognise it?

MAUD: *(Looking again)* No. Should I?

WILLIE: You were here once.

MAUD: Malloy's?

WILLIE: Before Malloy. *(He waits; she shakes her head)* This very room. Mrs Meredith?

MAUD: Nanny Meredith? No ..!

WILLIE: This was her sitting room.

MAUD: My God. It's so …

WILLIE: Malloy took all three cottages and knocked 'em through.

MAUD: She retired here, we came to see her, that summer.

WILLIE: We did. We sat in her sitting room and took tea and she told me all about you. And later, you told me, she took you on one side and asked in a whisper if we were engaged to be married ..?

MAUD: Hmm. And did I tell you what I answered?

WILLIE: I doubt it.

MAUD: I said Nanny Meredith, in every important respect I believe we are married already.

WILLIE: You said that? What did she say?

MAUD: She said O that's nice, Miss Gonne, I'm very happy for you. You'll recall she was three-quarters deaf, I don't believe she heard me.

WILLIE: Still, a beautiful thing to say.

MAUD: A beautiful thing to do. *(She gestures the room)* Thank you.

Silence. The saloon has grown more lively: fiddle, accordion, voice.

WILLIE: The day before that, Maud, the day before we came here.

MAUD: What about it?

WILLIE: …What did we do?

MAUD: Do? It was fifty years ago. What <u>did</u> we do?

WILLIE: I don't know, I'm asking <u>you</u> …

MAUD: … I don't <u>know</u>.

Standoff. They hardeye each other a moment.

MRS MALLOY: *(Arriving; the power behind the throne)* Ah good evening, good evening, nice to see you again, Mr Yeats, it's been a while, I have a card here to tempt a hawk from the sky but the beef and the lamb are both off and there's a special treat not on the card we call in the trade Sligo duck …

Willie's head jerks up from the card. Maud chuckles.

MRS MALLOY: … Oh, two gentlemen were asking after yez earlier on, sir, foreigners says Malloy but nice enough.

WILLIE: Foreigners? Where from?

MRS MALLOY: Malloy thought Dublin, I couldn't say.

The shot slides away, becomes a shot of two suited men sitting drinking in the saloon.

MAUD: Now this Sligo Duck, Mrs Malloy, what exactly would that be ..?

INT. SALOON BAR, FILLING UP.

Sweeney plays pot-boy, one of nature's oddjobbers. Approaches the two men's table. Waits for one of them to drain his glass. Goes to gather it. The man keeps his hand on the handle; gives Sweeney a hard stare. Sweeney's lips offer a disarming smile, but his eyes aren't in it.

Fiddle, accordion and voice set up in the far corner, picking up **Patrick was a Gentleman** *where Sweeney left it.*

SONG   … On the top of this high hill
           St Patrick preached his sermon
           Which drove the frogs into the bogs
           And banished all the vermin.
           There's not a mile of Eireann's isle
           Where dirty vermin musters
           But there he put his dear fore-foot
           And murdered them in clusters.

INT. PRIVATE ROOM. LATER.

Close shot of the skeletal remains of the sea bass on a salver. Mrs Malloy's hands lift the plate and place it on a side table by the wall.

MRS MALLOY: And how was the Sligo Duck then ..?

MAUD: *(Lighting cigarette)* Excellent, thank you.

WILLIE: *(Pouring coffee)* And mercifully nothing like a duck.

Mrs Malloy carries out. The din from the downstairs bar has grown more raucous, a fiddle has joined the music-makers.

MAUD: It's been a grand weekend, Willie.

WILLIE: When do you leave?

MAUD: I'll catch the twelve o'clock.

WILLIE: I'll let Sweeney know.

MAUD: I fear it hasn't helped you much.

WILLIE: Oh it has helped. I'm nearly there.

They drink their coffee in silence. Willie broods a little, working on things.

INT. SALOON BAR.

Sweeney stands drinking at the sidebar, his eyes on the two men. They check their watches, get up to leave. Sweeney drains his pot, drifts outside after them.

EXT. MALLOY'S BAR. ALMOST NIGHT.

The two men head for their car at the roadside. Sweeney tucks himself round a corner to take a leak and watch. The men board the car, squirt off up the hill towards the headland.

Sweeney buttons up, returns to the bar.

INT. SALOON BAR.

Across the crammed smoke-filled moil, Sweeney sees Willie in altercation at the bottom of the steps to the private room; moves at once to push his way through.

Cut to

INT. SALOON BAR, FAR PART OF ROOM, UNDER SIGN TO TOILETS.

A group of drunks have corralled the whitefaced Willie against the wall to snipe at him.

DRUNK 1: ... A cut above, is it, his high and mighty self in the fine suit ...

DRUNK 2: ... T'inks he knows more than the rest of us, got a fountain pen where his dick used to be ...

DRUNK 1: ... Couldn't tell his arse from his armpit, so he couldn't ...

DRUNK 2: ... An' niver done a decent day's work in his life ...

SWEENEY: *(Arriving; calm)* An' what would you know about a decent day's work, Pat O'Hare ..? *(To Willie)* Where's the lady?

Willie indicates Toilets, Sweeney nods, begins to clear a path. Maud appears. He waves her through, placing both behind him. Malloy comes out from behind the bar, Sweeney waves him still; in charge.

DRUNK 1: *(Some stout-sodden bluster)* Not your affair, Sweeney, keep yer nose to yerself if ye don't want it bustin' ...

SWEENEY: Shame on ye, Michael Finney, d'ye not know who this is ..?

DRUNK 1: I know who it is alright, it's mister bloody hoitytoity Yeats is who it is all right, he's ...

SWEENEY: ... Ireland's greatest poet is who he is, Michael Finney, and if he walks the high road to heaven and you crawl the gutters, that's maybe 'cause you haven't thought of standing upright like a man yet ... All right? *(The five men sway and snuffle, still dangerous)* I'll say one thing and then I'll go. Harm a hair of that man's head and I'll break ye in two, four, six, eight ... *(Reaches the last drunk)* ... ten. And I'll say another. Take yerselves to the bar there and have a glass on me.

Sweeney ushers Willie and Maud through the stilled room and out into the night.

EXT/INT. NIGHT. CAR.

Willie sits with his head back, eyes closed, still pale. Maud sits by him, her hand on his.

Sweeney sings, but more gently, picking up where the singer left off.

SWEENEY: The frogs went hop and the toads went pop
              Slapdash into the water
              And the snakes committed suicide ...

His headlamps pick up a parked car up ahead, its lights out. He stops the song to take in the two men up front, smoking cigarettes in the dark of the car.

SWEENEY: (On) ... To save themselves from slaughter.

He adjusts his rear-view mirror, picks up the car gathering speed behind them.

SWEENEY: Ah, there ye go, boys.

WILLIE: What?

SWEENEY: I think ye have company, sir.

WILLIE: Company?

Sweeney hoiks a thumb at the rear window. Willie hoists himself round to look into the glare of the car behind.

EXT. HOUSE. NIGHT.

Sweeney parks up by the side door as before. They sit in silence for a moment, waiting for the following car. Nothing.

SWEENEY: In we go then. *(He bips the horn, gets out at speed, opens the rear doors to help them out)* Lights, if you please ... *(The light goes on above the door)* Thank you.

Jane appears at the door, a torch in her hand.

JANE: There you are, come away inside, I've cocoa on the hob.

Lights rake the side of the house, the men's car rolls to a halt across the yard. The three stare at it through the glare.

JANE: Ah, you have company, sir.

The lights cut. The two men leave the car and approach at a saunter.

MAUD: Ah. Of course. S.B.

Sweeney gives her a look.

MAN: *(arrived)* I wonder if we might have a word with you, sir? *(He holds up his ID. Willie can't read it)* Inspector Lucan, Sergeant McShane. There's more light inside, sir, would ye mind ..?

WILLIE: And what business would you have with me, Inspector?

LUCAN: The business of the State, Senator.

WILLIE: The business of the State. *(A sniff)* Come in.

INT. PARLOUR. NIGHT.

Silence surrounds the ticking clock. Lucan and McShane sit in armchairs, side by side. Maud sits opposite, sipping whiskey. McShane reaches for her manuscript memoir, which has now found its way onto the parlour table. Studies the front. Shows it to Lucan, who nods.

Sounds of toilet flushing, Willie appears, buttoning flies.

WILLIE: You won't have reached your prostrates yet, gentlemen, but you will. *(Plumping into his chair)* Now tell me one thing, Inspector. Do I look like a man who would be hiding an escaped Volunteer in his summer house?

LUCAN: No no, of course not, sir.

He looks deliberately at Maud, who returns the stare.

WILLIE: ... I am William Butler Yeats, founder and president of the Irish National Theatre, Nobel Prize winner, eight years a Senator in the Dail, I have – if you'll pardon the expression – done this State some service.

LUCAN: We're simply acting on information, sir, and bound to check it out.

WILLIE: Information. Mm. Well, you've done your duty, there is no such person on these premises ...

LUCAN: I'm sure there isn't, sir, would you mind if we checked ..?

WILLIE: *(Popping)* Are you saying I'm a liar, sir?

MAUD: Easy, Willie, the Inspector's only doing his job … Special Branch has all our interests at heart.

Lucan gives her another searching look. She smiles sweetly.

LUCAN: Would you mind if we took a brief tour of the house, Senator? Just so's we can tell the office we done a search?

WILLIE: You have a warrant?

LUCAN: We can get one.

WILLIE: Come back when you have it. *(Stands)* Anything else?

LUCAN: *(unbudging)* One or two things, yes.

WILLIE: I need my pills.

He leaves the room. The two men fix their attention on Maud, who's lighting a cigarette. Lucan gives McShane a nod.

MCSHANE: 'A Servant of the Queen'? This yours, Madam?

MAUD: It is, in a manner of speaking. Though it's the Senator's copy.

MCSHANE: And this word in pencil on the front, ma'am.

MAUD: Yes?

MCSHANE: Finnegan, does it say?

MAUD: *(Taking a look)* It might. It could be Finnegan. I know Mr Yeats was talking long-distance with Joyce yesterday.

MCSHANE: *(Pencil ready)* Joyce who?

MAUD: James Joyce. *(The two men stare blankly at her)* The novelist. I believe he has a work-in-progress about a funeral.

LUCAN: What's this to do with Finnegan?

MAUD: I believe he's the main character. He's thinking of calling it Finnegan's Funeral.

MCSHANE: *(copying it all down)* … Funeral. Mm. Where can we find this … *(Checks notes)* Joyce feller?

MAUD: Paris.

Silence.

MCSHANE: *(obdurate)* So that's not your handwriting at all then.

A muffled cry from the Library across the way. They turn to look. Sweeney speeds past from the kitchen. Maud stands, moves to see what's happening.

Sees

IN LIBRARY.

Sweeney crouches over Willie's prone body on the carpet, his pill bottle near his hand, pills everywhere.

MAUD: My God, is he all right?

SWEENEY: *(Fingers on neck-pulse)* He's breathing, ma'am.

MAUD: *(At desk, clicking phone rest for operator)* Doctor doctor doctor … *(She sees the SB men in the doorway)* I think you might usefully leave the premises now, gentlemen, you've probably been instrumental in seeing off Ireland's greatest man of letters, a fine night's work and one I'm sure the Minister of Justice will want to hear all about … Hello, hello … Yes, this is the summer house. Out on the head there, yes, we need Mr Yeats' doctor urgently, ahunh, yes, thank you …

She replaces the receiver, joins Sweeney on the rug. A car starts up outside, lights sweep the trees, they're gone.

WILLIE: *(From nowhere)* Are the buggers gone?

Maud and Sweeney look at each other. Willie draws himself to the sit.

WILLIE: Damn 'em, they'd've stayed all night, sniffing for bones. Good, eh? Should've been an actor. It's a gift, you know. Give me a hand.

Sweeney hands him upright with a chuckle.

MAUD: You bugger. I thought you were a goner.

WILLIE: Me? I'll live forever, didn't I tell you? *(The pills)* Gather those up will ye Mr Sweeney, I'll only tread them into the carpet, I'm on my way …

MAUD: I'll walk you up.

SWEENEY: Leave it to me, Your Grace, you get yourself a mug of cocoa.

WILLIE: I wouldn't mind a mug meself.

MAUD: I'll bring you one up.

She leaves for the kitchen. Sweeney helps Willie to the stairs and up; for the moment, comrades-in-arms. The pace is weirdly slow, as if the collapse had been real.

SWEENEY: *(As they recede)* Is it still actin' y'are or what, sir?

WILLIE: *(Eventually)* Guess.

INT. KITCHEN.

Jane cuts sandwiches: bread, cheese, pickle. Swings round tense-eyed as Maud enters.

JANE: Ah it's you, mum, come for your cocoa.

MAUD: And a mug for the Man Himself, if ye would.

She sits, suddenly drained. Notes the substantial pile of sandwiches down the table. Can't make sense of it.

JANE: *(At the hob with the mugs)* Did Finbar speak with you at all, mum? Sweeney.

MAUD: Finbar. Lovely name. No, what about?

JANE: He'll tell ye himself soon enough, mum.

She stirs the milk and cocoa, fills the bold blue dolphin-motif mugs.

MAUD: Mr Sweeney was wonderful this evening, down there at the bar. Spoke up for the Man in a roomful of drunks and faced them down with a surprising passion. *(The sandwiches)*

JANE: A passionate man, mum. And not the fool he looks.

(Sweeney's heavy clump on the stair, returning at speed). It's his feet's his achilles heel …

SWEENEY: Did you tell her, love? *(Jane shakes her head)* Go and ring the doctor, will you, tell him false alarm, the Great Man's fine.

He squeezes her hand as she passes. She blushes a little smile. He crosses to the hob, pours himself a cocoa.

SWEENEY: The man who phoned earlier, ma'am.

MAUD: Yes.

SWEENEY: … said he might come out here.

MAUD: Yes.

SWEENEY: Finnegan, was it?

MAUD: I believe it was.

SWEENEY: He's in the coalhouse. Came while we were out.

MAUD: Mm. *(She looks inside her bag, closes it).* I'd better go and see him. *(Pointing down passage to outside door)* It's that way, isn't it?

SWEENEY: I'll take you through, Ma'am …

MAUD: Your goodness will lead you to the grave, Mr Sweeney, this is not your concern.

SWEENEY: We'll need a torch.

He collects one from a ledge, leads off down the passage.

EXT. SIDE OF HOUSE. MOONLIT NIGHT, SCUDDING CLOUD.

Sweeney scans the driveway and trees, Maud just behind him. Nothing. He points his torch to the ground behind him, sets off down the side of the house, lighting Maud's footing.

He stops, torch cut, scents the air; a feral creature still somewhere inside him. Moves on.

INT. COALHOUSE, NIGHT.

Sounds of bolts being drawn, the door pushes open, the torch lances the barn of a space, picking out heaps of logs and mounds of coal.

SWEENEY: Are ye there now, sirrah? *(Nothing)* I'm Sweeney, twas my wife hid ye here. *(Nothing)* I've Miss Gonne here with me.

Silence, then small sounds of someone emerging from spread tarpaulin. The torch finds him; brings him out. He's maybe 17, a baby-faced runt of a kid, hard masking scared.

Maud passes Sweeney into the space, takes the torch from him.

MAUD: Thank you, Mr Sweeney. That will be all for the moment.

SWEENEY: I'll step outside then, will I?

She nods. He steps outside. Maud moves in to the space. The boy shimmers in the moonwashed dark.

MAUD: I don't know who you are, who sent you, what you've done, why you're on the run to England. I do this because I can do no other. *(She opens her bag, hands him the letter)* This will help you find a place to stay. *(She opens her purse, hands him some cash.)* This'll help you get there.

The kid takes both, pockets them, his eyes fixed on the woman in front of him.

FINNEGAN: Are you really Maud Gonne? *(He shakes his head)* S'like meetin' the Virgin Mary. Hell fire, wait till I tell the boys, will they be green.

Maud watches the tremble in his shoulders, smells the fear.

MAUD: I wish you Godspeed. You'll cope.

FINNEGAN: Miss.

MAUD: What is it?

FINNEGAN: Would you pray with me?

MAUD: If ye will.

The lad kneels, Maud joins him. They pray in silence. The boy gulps. Maud looks at him. He's crying.

She puts her arm round his scrawny back, he puts his head on her shoulder, tears mottle his pinched face.

Cut to

INT. HOUSE. STAIRWAY TO FIRST FLOOR.

Maud climbs the stairs, Willie's cocoa in her hand; sees Sweeney at the top cutting his toenails on a newspaper.

SWEENEY: All done are we, ma'am?

MAUD: You're a foolish brave man, Finbar Sweeney, so you are. *(She stoops, places a kiss on his head)* Good night.

She swishes past him and on towards the second flight. Sweeney sits on, his whole frame sexualised by the kiss and the contact, his eyes closed.

SWEENEY: *(Eventually; after her)* Pleasant dreams, milady.

INT. UPPER STAIRWAY.

Light spills from Willie's open door as Maud approaches the stairhead landing.

WILLIE: *(From within)* Bring my cocoa did ye ..?

MAUD: You should be asleep, you old witch.

She looks in. Sees

INT. WORKROOM.

Willie's at work in the middle of a set-up, stretching and fixing a bolt of sky-blue silk along a wall. There are candles, signs, pictures ranged around the silk wall.

He's alive, tireless, deep in what he does.

MAUD: *(Laying mug down)* Shouldn't you sleep?

WILLIE: Go to bed.

MAUD: I'll sleep …

WILLIE: Thank you.

MAUD: Thank you, Willie.

They look at each other across the crazy room. He raises his fingers to his lips, sends her a kiss.

MAUD: Will I see you before I leave?

WILLIE: *(A grin)* You might. *(She's leaving. He waits till she's all but gone)* Maud. *(She turns)* That summer, here at Howth, the day before ..? We crossed the bay and climbed Long Hill and near the top we lay in the high heather and looked into the sky together and envisioned … remember ..?

MAUD: Nothing. No.

WILLIE: … The Castle …

MAUD: I don't remember.

WILLIE: The Place of Heroes. Yes.

Silence.

MAUD: No, Willie.

She crosses to her room, closes the door.

Willie turns back to his work. Sits lotus-legged before the blue silk sky. Gazes into the silk. Sounds begin a slow bubble deep in the body.

Willie's face, close up, the eyes filled with blue.

His point of view: a sky-blue screen.

Intercut, snap shots of the house:

Finnigan, smoking a cigarette, on his back, staring out through the skylight.

Sweeney lying in Jane's arms between the sheets, sleeping like a child. Jane strokes his head.

Ext shot of the house, angled to show outline against cloud-streaked sky.

Overhead of Maud in her bed, drifting towards sleep.

Willie again, eyes driving in, on.

The blue skyscreen.

FINAL VISION

EXT. LONG HILL, HOWTH. SUMMER DAY.

Willie and Maud, mid-thirties, lie on their backs in the high heather, staring at the big bare sky.

WILLIE: *(Over, from trance)* Yes? *(No answer)* Yes?

On the reverse, we see the sky they see.

WILLIE: *(Over, from trance)* Water first, then fire. Now air … Yes!

The sky they watch becomes

LOUGH KEY, LATE EVENING.

Painted and gilded oars dip and lift, the boat moves relentlessly on towards the island castle ahead. Held flambeaux light the smouldery way.

Shot of the pair, Maud at the prow, Willie at the stern, alone in the moving boat, torch-lit, staring ahead. Between them, a raised black coffin draped with an Irish flag.

WILLIE: Yes yes yes … This is it. This is it, Maud.

EXT. ISLAND. DARKENING SKY.

Long shot of the two on the shingle beach, the burning torches now in their hands, gazing up at the mouldering castle. The boat has evaporated; dreamed out.

INT/EXT. CASTLE.

They walk the ruined rooms in silence, torches raised. Above them, broad sweeps of starlit sky through the crumbled roofs.

WILLIE: *(Over, from trance)* That's right! All was open and open to the sky. Save one last room.

Shot of squat sunken oak door, a short flight of stone steps leading down. Maud approaches, Willie behind her; they read an inscription on the metal plaque driven into the wood: **Locus Futuri/ Porta exire singuli.**

WILLIE: *(Over, from trance)* The Room of the Future. Pass one by one …

Maud pushes against the door to open it. Offers Willie entry, he waves her on, she stoops to pass into the dark, the door swings shut behind her.

Willie approaches the door, pushes; it stays shut. He bangs the wood with his palms, calling her name.

WILLIE: *(Over, from trance) Take me, Maud. Take me inside. Take me with you.*
   Show me what you saw.

MAUD: *(Over, from dream) … I saw nothing.*

WILLIE: *(Over, from trance) Show me …*

Abrupt cut to

INT. ROOM OF THE FUTURE.

Maud stands, back to the door, in the black hole, torch raised. Behind her,
echoic light years away, Willie's voice calls her name.

MAUD: *(Over, from dream) Why, Willie? Let it be.*

WILLIE: *(Over, from trance) The last vision. The last room. Maud?*

Shot of the flap of flame of her torch against the unpenetrated blackness of the
space.

Sound builds in the black void: air in movement; unearthly.

An island of light grows slowly at the heart of the void, reveals a perfect circle
of tessellated floor, a marble tomb at its centre.

WILLIE: *(Over, from trance) Ah. Ah.*

Shot of Maud on her back on the tomb, staring up into the light. In her point of
view, we see only intense white light, too strong to source.

Her face, rapt. The light slowly dims.

Her point of view again: a vast star-packed sky, at once real and planetarial,
begins to define itself in the resuming dark.

MAUD: *(Over, from dream) No more, Willie …*

WILLIE: *(Over, from trance) More. Everything.*

The sky explodes.

Images of the century we've lived, mute actuality footage of the century she
faces, early and late promiscuously bundled, cut for speed not sense, cascade
from deep space: a one hundred-second catalogue of one hundred years of war
and destruction and famine and horror and deep global self-abuse; a sort of Old
Testament of our times, probably set down by Jeremiah; your list as good as
anyone's and not a pretty sight.

WILLIE: *(Over, throughout, from trance) Everything. Everything. Everything.*
   Everything. Everything.

The last image: an on-board shot of a 3000lb Cruise missile mapping its way
through suburban Baghdad, 100 feet from the ground, en route.

WILLIE: *(Over, from trance, a whisper) Everything, Maud.*

Fast cut to

EXT. LONG HILL, HOWTH HEAD. SUMMER DAY.

Tightening vertical downshot of the pair on their backs in the high heather a hundred feet below.

Their voices drift up. As the shot closes in, we hear them.

WILLIE: If you will not marry me, at least …

MAUD: At least let you have me? Is that what you mean?

Willie props himself up on an elbow to look at her.

WILLIE: Maud, I want you all. I want every last hair of you, cell of you, smell of you. I want everything.

MAUD: You don't want everything, Willie. You want my sex. That's the everything you want, am I right?

Willie stares down at her, stunned, uncertain. She begins quietly unbuttoning her blouse and bodice. Breasts begin to appear.

MAUD: Come then. We'll make love, will we.

She draws him gently to her, brushes her lips on his, draws his head to her breasts. He shivers, moans, trembles, everything inside him struggling to release.

He comes almost at once, well short of everything, on a long hopeless groan, half joy, half shame.

Maud strokes his head. Willie lies back from her. Covers his wettening crotch with a spread hand.

MAUD: *(Over, from dream)Oh Willie. Was it so important?*

Sometimes enough is everything.

VISION ENDS

Cut to

EXT. EARLY MORNING.

Shot of the house from the sea. Gulls wind on the wind.

INT. HOUSE.

Maud washes herself at the basin by the window, ready for the day. The flannel dips between her legs, her body at ease with itself.

Cut to

INT. WILLIE'S STUDY.

Willie sleeps fully-dressed on his camp-bed by the wall; out to the world. A smile comes and goes on his lips.

Moving to

EXT. MIDMORNING.

Sweeney bangs the banger down the hill to Howth. Maud hangs on.

SWEENEY: *(Singing)*

>   Nine hundred thousand reptiles blue
>   He charmed with sweet discourses
>   And dined on them in Killaloe
>   On soups and second courses …

Moving to

INT. TRAIN BACK TO DUBLIN.

Maud stares at the sea through the window of the carriage.

WILLIE: *(Letter voice over)* … I am gone at last to France, a last time, I know I will not be back. I have found no way of using the visions you shared with me in Howth. I know now there will be a war and another and another, I can say nothing, my war ended long ago and I will hold my tongue.

The window reflection suddenly becomes a flash-image of an Irish naval frigate arriving in Cork Harbour, a black coffin on deck draped in the Irish Flag.

Cut to

EXT. GARDEN, SOUTH OF FRANCE. MORNING.

Willie sits wrapped in a rug, writing the letter, clearly less well.

WILLIE: *(Letter-voice over)* … As to the other thing, my hitherto unspeakable sexual prematurity, how can it be important, what you gave me was always enough and everything …

Moving to

EXT. MAUD'S GARDEN. EVENING.

She sits at the long table surrounded by animals, reading his letter.

WILLIE: *(Letter-voice over)* You were the luck I had, Maud. See the enclosed poem. The last.

She feels in the envelope, finds the poem.

Cut to

EXT. FRIGATE. CORK HARBOUR, 1948.

A military band plays the Dead March as the coffin is shouldered onto the quayside. State, church and military dignitaries wait above the crowd to receive the body back from France.

WILLIE: *(Poem-voice over)*

>   How can I, that girl standing there,
>   My attention fix
>   On Roman or on Russian
>   Or on Spanish politics?
>   Yet here's a travelled man that knows
>   What he talks about,
>   And there's a politician

That has read and thought,
And maybe what they say is true
Of war and war's alarms,
But O that I were young again
And held her in my arms …

Captions in:

William Butler Yeats died as predicted a few months later. the war delayed the return of his body to Ireland until 1948, when it was received at Cork Harbour on behalf of the nation by Seán MacBride, Minister for External Affairs and Maud's son.

Maud Gonne MacBride, for whom the war never ended, died in 1953 at the age of 91. It isn't known what she thought of Willie's last poem.

Ireland is still at war.

END

Reviews

Direct Democracy

Boaventura de Sousa Santos (editor), *Democratizing Democracy: Beyond the Liberal Democratic Canon*, Verso Publications, 512 pages, ISBN 9781844671472, £24.99

This collection of articles ably edited by Boaventura de Sousa Santos is consciously perceived as the first in a series of five such books dealing with the issue of 'Reinventing Social Emancipation'. The other four volumes will be thematically organized around 'alternative production systems', 'emancipatory multiculturalism, cultural justice and citizenship', 'protection of biodiversity and recognition of local knowledges', and 'new labour internationalism', respectively. This volume is about 'participatory democracy' or why it is necessary and possible to move from a 'low intensity democracy' to a 'high intensity' one. The latter is characterized by a much stronger presence of forms of participatory democracy that complement and combine with the representative forms associated with a liberal democracy in which, unfortunately, the liberal dimension has always been much more important than the democratic dimension.

Why is such a shift of discourse and practice necessary? This is because the actual history of the hegemonic form of democracy – a proceduralist representative one – has proved itself to be incapable of resolving the growing economic, political, social, cultural and ecological problems of our times. Indeed, its own trajectory is one of diminishing value. Even as liberal democracy has spread in the post-Cold War era, it has thinned everywhere including in its Western European and North American bastions. This is hardly surprising considering its connection to the worldwide extension of neoliberalism as the dominant form of economic globalization. But why is such a shift at all possible? The strength of this volume is that it seeks to answer this question in the affirmative in two ways.

The first approach is on the theoretical level in which basic assumptions of the proceduralist conception of democracy – the impossibility of any significant role for forms of direct democracy once the scale and complexity of the governed space increases; the indispensability of specialized bureaucracies as providers of knowledge and expertise; the unavoidability of authorization only through representation – are assaulted. The second approach is through the presentation and evaluation of the experiences of social movements of emancipation and the structures of local participation that they have given rise to in five countries. Four of the countries were chosen not simply because they represented the three third world continents but because they are semi-peripheral countries of intermediate level industrialization. According to the editor, experiments in participatory democracy have been strongest in such semi-peripheral countries. The fifth country – Mozambique – is a peripheral country chosen to present a counterpoint but also no doubt because the editor has a specific familiarity with it. The overall result, as is to be expected from such compilations, is a certain unevenness of quality and relevance. One of the best parts of the book is the introductory chapter by Santos and Leonardo Avritzer, which is the theoretical critique of what they call the 'hegemonic liberal democratic' model.

To put one's faith in purely representative democracy and centralized bureaucracies, they say, is actually to deny oneself the very creativity in the use of information/knowledge that comes from its inevitably dispersed nature. It is to deny oneself the greater responsiveness to publicly articulated needs and concerns that is possible, as well as the greater efficacy in policy implementation that more decentralized and participatory forms of democracy can provide. Representative democracy may resolve the problem of authorization, but it cannot be sufficiently sensitive to the need for high levels of accountability nor can it assure proper respect and articulation of the concerns of minority identities. And *contra* Isaiah Berlin, value pluralism does not mean that the essence of democracy must forever be a proceduralism or that it can never be structured in ways that promote a 'common good'. Here Habermas's work on the importance of a deliberative democracy, of a public space and of rational discourse provides an important counter and corrective to the dominant liberal democratic discourse. Habermas connects the principle of participation and representation in a deeper synthesis. Indeed, participatory budgeting as in Brazil and elsewhere is a real-life validation of his claims. Ultimately, Santos and Avritzer remind us that democracy is not primarily about the restriction of state power but about the disalienation of social power, be it the power of patriarchy in the household, exploitative power in the workplace, identity hierarchies in the community-space, the fetishism of commodities in the marketplace, or unequal exchange in the world-space.

When it comes to the various case studies it is not quite clear why two chapters are devoted to each of the other four countries while Colombia gets five chapter treatments. These case studies are divided into four parts. The first part is titled 'Social Movements and Democratic Aspirations'. Part two is titled 'Women's Struggle for Democracy'. Part three is totally devoted to democratic struggles in Colombia despite its ongoing civil war. And part four is about 'Participatory Democracy in Action'. In part one, D.L. Sheth provides an overview of how in India certain social movements in the 1990s have sought to counter the promotion of neoliberal globalization by urban élites and, in doing so, have encouraged various practices of participatory democracy. These are movements that are linked to indigenous traditions, both of Gandhianism and of left social democracy. These have opposed the destructive impulses of development, the distortions of discourse, and the socio-economic inequalities that have all been fostered by current globalization. These movements constitute rays of hope but are encased within a wider trajectory that shows no signs of deviating away from neoliberalism, and this tends to undercut Sheth's own optimism about the future.

Sakhela Buhlungu explains how and why grassroots democratic bodies that sprang up during the struggle against apartheid have declined and degenerated in the post-apartheid era. The writer's assessment is reinforced in another chapter by Shamim Meer appearing in part two that explains why white women have benefited most from the struggle for gender equality in South Africa. The key problem in both cases has been that the end of apartheid came about through a negotiated pact between two élites that led to a restructuring of the political sphere without any restructuring of the economic sphere. What is more, the top leaders of the African National Congress were people in prisons or in exile long separated from the day-to-day involvement in the grassroots movements and struggles, less controlled by them and thus more susceptible to the material temptations and rewards that could come to them as a result of their ascendance after the political transition.

Two pieces on the strengths and limitations of women's struggles in Mozambique by Conceicao Osorio and Maria Jose Arthur are informative certainly but hardly encouraging in that the Women's Committees in Mozambique seem to have become firmly subordinated to party dictates. The female leadership of these Committees, rather than challenging the predominantly male party hierarchy and ethos, seems to have settled for a 'promotion of women' through the standard route of putting in more female faces in the higher echelons rather than trying to achieve more substantive transformations in the relationship between the sexes in the political parties and in their front organizations.

The coverage of Colombia is of course the most comprehensive. Rodrigo Uprimny and Mauricio Garcia Villegas describe the role of the Constitutional Court in the 1990s. This Court gave strong judicial support to the rights of indigenous people and to the middle class debtors' movement. There are some acute observations about the strengths and weaknesses of such judicial activism and its relationship to social emancipation. The struggle of coca planters and harvesters, in 1996, in the western region of Colombia is graphically portrayed by Maria Ramirez. This struggle enabled these marginalized and targeted communities to achieve a new dignity. Their very success in getting a government, which had been committed to arbitrarily and forcibly destroying their crops, to negotiate with them and to discuss alternative cropping arrangements was a decisive form of self-empowerment and dignity enhancement.

Elsewhere, despite the ultimate decay of the peoples' militias comprising poor youth in the drug capital of Medellin, Francisco-Gutierrez Sanin and Ana Maria Jaramillo show how they did nevertheless play for a long time a remarkable role in containing criminal mafia gangs. In the Uraba region, banana workers allied with left guerrillas to strengthen their union and, having achieved a significant stature, began negotiating with banana producers from a new position of strength. A new set of relationships then emerged in which steady material progress could now be obtained through the institutionalization of collective bargaining mechanisms and principles. This required moving away from the FARC while the other main guerrilla group, the EPL, had abandoned armed struggle by the early 1990s and become partially incorporated within the existing structures of political and class power. Here, Mauricio Romero paints a complex picture of how substantial cooptation becomes the price paid by the banana workers for real benefits that otherwise would not have been achieved.

The case studies that are most inspiring and represent the most advanced experiences of sustained participatory democracy are left for the last part of the book. Maria Teresa Uribe gives us the story of how the citizens of San Jose de Apartado, strategically situated in the foothills of the Aribe mountain range (whose upper reaches were the safe havens of the FARC), were caught in the crossfire of the bitter armed conflict between the army and paramilitaries on one side and the FARC on the other. These citizens first decided, in 1996, to move towards a declaration of neutrality in this conflict and then, in 1997, to publicly declare themselves a 'community of peace'. This did not make them immune to armed assaults (mostly from the side of the army/paramilitaries). But theirs is nonetheless an inspiring story of courage, resilience and persistence. International recognition as a 'community of peace' from various sources – universities, municipalities, governments, non-governmental organizations – all helped eventually to provide a measure of protection and a *de facto* recognition of this universally appreciated community self-description by both warring sides. But this 'community of peace' could not have sustained itself as it did without creating a collective unity that extended beyond issues of protection to a collective reorganization of production and of the functions of everyday life, becoming thereby an unexpected model of participatory democracy.

Santos and Avritzer tell us about the principles, practices and lessons of participatory budgeting (PB) first in Porto Alegre and then of its extension to other cities in Brazil. Although much already has been written about PB, we have yet to arrive at a full balance-sheet of its strengths and limitations. The enduring success of PB in Porto Alegre is based on the actualization of three key principles – every adult can participate; the structure of decision-making involves an institutionalized combination of direct and indirect representative rules; investment resources are allocated by objective criteria that combine general concerns and technical considerations. The overall result is that PB has made a genuine and real difference in the lives of people; it has respected their priorities and ranking of needs.

Much the same can be said of the experience of decentralised planning through the Panchayati Raj system in the state of Kerala in India. This is a three-tier administrative system operating at the ward and village level, at the level of a block comprising, say, 100 villages, and then the district comprising several blocks. The state itself is made up of several districts. The experience of Kerala is recounted by Patrick Heller and T.H. Thomas Isaac, who has been a key participant and activist leader in the People's Campaign of 1996 that sought to bring about this decentralized planning system wherein the state government now allocates some 40% of its total budget to the Panchayati Raj system and control over which is bottom-up rather than top-down. As in Porto Alegre and elsewhere, there is no doubt that this system has led to real improvement in meeting locally determined basic needs. But what the authors on Kerala have not pointed out is that this decentralized planning has also shown itself inadequate when it comes to longer term development and planning for the state as a whole or for its separate regions and localities.

But the larger issues have to do with how generalizable these experiences of advanced democratic decentralization are to other parts of the world and how effective they can be in promoting a bottom-up revamping of political and economic macro-spheres. In regard to the first issue, it is true that the prior existence of strong grassroots social movement-type organizations was crucial for the initiation of such experiments. There was the Worker's Party or PT in Brazil and the powerful Peoples'

Science Movement or KSSP in Kerala. But even so, the structures that have emerged, and the principles of organization on which they are based, have been transportable and their very implantation in different soils has on occasions itself generated the kind of public enthusiasm that makes them sustainable in the longer run.

The main problem, however, is that it is both unclear and extraordinarily difficult to see how such forms of participatory democracy can be pushed upwards; how such decentralized mechanisms can become the springboard to transform the centralized and national-level apparatuses. Thus, in both Brazil and India, the overall economic direction remains firmly neoliberal and macro-level democratic practices almost purely representative. Thus it affords insufficient satisfaction that Emir Sader in a final concluding chapter that ably sums up all the contributions should confidently and correctly declare that the most advanced forms of participatory democracy can combine 'institutionalized embeddedness and the constant processes of popular mobilization'. The most important strategic-political question for carrying out a truly radical transformation at the macro-level remains unanswered in this volume. How do we effectively link the politics of the singular and particular with the politics of the national and universal? Historically, the main organizational form that such a successful combination has taken has been the revolutionary party, whose fortunes currently appear rather dim. But a 'radical pluralism' aiming to stitch together various separate expressions of identity politics or different social movements focused on specific sectoral concerns has so far proved unimpressive as a possible organizational alternative. But these unanswered dilemmas are no reason for being ungrateful for the insights that have been offered in this volume.   *Achin Vanaik*

Recent Times

Mark Garnett, *From Anger to Apathy: The British Experience Since 1975*, Jonathan Cape, 480 pages, ISBN13 978-0224073066, £20

In February 2003, millions of people in some 800 cities world-wide took part in global protests against the imminent invasion of Iraq by the military forces of the United States and the United Kingdom. In England, people from all over the country gathered in London. There was a separate gathering in Scotland, in Glasgow. The BBC said over 500,000 people attended the London demonstration, while the Stop the War Coalition, which organised the day, put the number at two million. Whatever the assessments, it is safe to say that the march was amongst the largest political demonstrations ever seen in Britain. Did these protests influence decisions taken in Westminster? We hear, in reply, a resounding 'no'! Why, then, should the voting public remain active in the political process if their well-publicised concerns are ignored in this way?

Apathy, annoyance and mistrust of politics are key issues in Mark Garnett's *From Anger to Apathy: The British Experience Since 1975*. The author examines whether there has been a change in the British people's attitude to politics over the last three decades. Has apathy increased whilst anger has diminished, since the mid 1970s? Is the British public more 'passive consumer' than 'active citizen'? To answer these questions Garnett charts the media's involvement in politics and political involvement in the media during these decades.

The author refers to a variety of television programmes, politically charged rock bands, and tabloid and broadsheet newspapers throughout *From Anger to Apathy*. This helps to situate his narrative for those of us who were growing up during these years. His main source is *The Times* newspaper, which he has subjected to close scrutiny during the years from 1975 to the present. For Garnett, media-led moral panics and exposés of political scandal have been relatively new features of journalism since 1975.

In his view, the media's ability to embarrass the government of the day, and whip people into a frenzy, reflect a decline in journalistic practice. In the 1970s, politicians began to be held in contempt more widely as a result of scandals such as that caused by John Stonehouse, the former Postmaster General in the Wilson Government, who made an unsuccessful attempt at faking his own death. Later, during the 1980s, anger surrounded the long awaited miners' strike of 1984. According to Garnett, the media managed to portray the most militant miners as 'the scum of the earth'(p. 110). They found a photo of the miners' leader, Arthur Scargill, in a pose that was made to appear as though he was giving a Nazi-style salute. This 'doctoring' of the miners' dispute aided the Conservatives' closure of many pits in Britain during that decade.

Later still, in July 1994, *The Sunday Times* revealed that Conservative MPs had been paid £1,000 for 'tabling parliamentary questions'. The tables were turned; where reporting had once favoured and assisted the government of the day in their policies, there was now a surge of damning articles.

Faith in the British political system has been shaken over the last three decades, according to Garnett. The resulting low turn-out of eligible voters in the 2001 General Election is, for the author, an expression of the belief held by many UK voters that it makes little or no difference to their lives who is in power.

From Anger to Apathy is a readable and lively account of British politics from 1975 onwards. The author gives facts and figures, mainly taken from *The Times* or other newspaper sources, but never critically analyses the information, nor the epochs in question. Given that his survey observes the 'decline in journalistic practice' and the permissive use of the media by politicians and politicians by the media, it seems unwise to base most of his research on the very medium he disparages. This and the lack of critical analysis detract from an otherwise engaging read.   *Abi Rhodes*

How Did David Kelly Die?

Norman Baker MP, *The Strange Death of David Kelly*, **Methuen, 400 pages, ISBN 9781842752173, £9.99**

In 2006, Norman Baker resigned his position as a Liberal Democrat front bench spokesman on environmental issues to devote himself to investigating the events surrounding the death, on 17 July 2003, of Britain's chief weapons inspector, Dr. David Kelly. He did this because he doubted the official explanation of death by suicide and wrote an article, in July 2006, in the *Mail on Sunday* expressing his concerns and asking for responses. As a result he received many hundreds of letters, e-mails and phone calls, all but three supporting his decision to publish his concerns.

The concerns were well based. On 7 January 2004, the *Guardian* newspaper had published a letter from three specialist medical professionals questioning the verdict of suicide. This was followed by further letters from health professionals expressing their doubts about the official explanation of Dr. Kelly's death, and about the way in which the inquiry by Lord Hutton into the affair had been conducted. Norman Baker adds further doubts about a man considering suicide. Dr. Kelly had just booked an early flight back to Iraq; his wife was unwell and, despite some indications of worry, he had appeared quite cheerful to those who saw him earlier on the day of his death

Only one day after Dr. Kelly's death, and after talking with the Prime Minster who was in Japan or *en route* for Japan, the Lord Chancellor had approached Lord Hutton, a one-time Lord Chief Justice of Northern Ireland, to head up an informal inquiry into the death. This was a somewhat unusual decision since it pre-empted the normal inquest on a death being carried out by the local coroner. It was a matter of some importance because, unlike a coroner's inquest, Lord Hutton's inquiry did not require witnesses to attend, nor to give evidence on oath, nor to submit to cross-examination. In fact, the inquest was stopped for the inquiry and not resumed thereafter, despite the willingness of the coroner to do so.

Lord Hutton justified this informal procedure in an article in the *Inner Temple Yearbook, 2004/5* by writing that:

'the basic facts which led to the tragic death of Dr. Kelly were already apparent from reports in the press and other parts of the media. Therefore I thought that there would be little serious dispute as to the background facts … I thought that unnecessary time could be taken by cross-examination on matters which were not directly relevant.'

Norman Baker's comment is 'As in controversial cases where he had presided in the past [i.e. in Northern Ireland — MBB] one could conjecture that Lord Hutton appeared, to a large degree, to have made up his mind in advance'. And what Lord Hutton had summarised in his report was:

'in the light of the evidence which I have heard I am satisfied that Dr. Kelly took his own life in the wood at Harrowdown Hill at a time between 4.15 p.m. on 17th July and 1.15 a.m. on 18th July 2003, and that the principal cause of death was bleeding from incised wounds to the left wrist which Dr. Kelly inflicted upon himself with the knife found beside the body.'

This summary conclusion was reached in spite of several pieces of conflicting evidence. The body was said by different witnesses to have been found lying face down, propped up on a tree or, alternatively, half twisted and curled up to one side. Dr Kelly was said to have been seen leaving his house for his constitutional walk on the fatal day without a coat but was found dead in the wood with a coat on. The number of police officers present varied, some said to have been in black, and some in blue. The small amount of blood on the ground was not suggestive of a cut artery and the blood stained water bottle seemed to be propped up out of Dr. Kelly's reach. Two empty packets of co-codamol were found in his coat pocket, but no pills in his stomach when autopsied.

Then who killed David Kelly and how was it done? There were plenty of Saddam Hussein's men who would like to have got him out of the way, but why do it in England and not in Iraq when he was there? The US and British governments, who had launched a war on Iraq on the pretext that Saddam had weapons of mass destruction ready for use at 45 minutes' notice, had every reason to fear that Dr. Kelly would reveal more of his doubts about this pretext, which he had already begun to suggest to the BBC correspondent, Andrew Gilligan. If the British secret service was responsible, that would explain the immediate decision to have an inquiry in a safe pair of hands and not an inquest by an uncontrollable coroner. Such an explanation is given added authority by the erection during the body's examination at the site of death of an enormously tall radio mast required only for communication half way across the world – to Japan, perhaps, or to an aeroplane *en route* for Japan or to the United States.

US involvement would be understandable enough, after the invasion of Iraq, and is given some credence by the extraordinary fact that the chief constable of the Thames Valley police force, which was responsible for the local inquiries into the death, on leaving the force two years later, won a US award for special police services, never previously awarded to a non-US citizen.

The manner of Dr.Kelly's death is, on the face of it, more difficult to understand. But, apparently, as Norman Baker discovered, there are chemical substances which, when introduced into the human body, can destroy life without leaving any trace behind. How exactly this was done in Dr. Kelly's case remained a mystery until Norman Baker received information from a source whom he came to trust but promised not to reveal by so much as a hint.

The story was that David Kelly was seized on his walk but outside the wood where his body was found. His house was raided and the coat and pills and knife and water bottle taken away with the body to be set up in the wood as they were discovered some hours later. To get the body to this site, without being seen, a boat had to be used on the nearby River Thames. The whole job was perhaps made to look amateurish in order to conceal its professional origins, which seem to have involved people from Iraq but with British associations. Three men were certainly noticed in a boat on the river at the time and the behaviour of the police was in many ways most peculiar. First of all, the entry in the police records for the whole affair was dated from a time before David Kelly was known to have died. Secondly, there was the delay in the police arrival on the scene after the body was found, and the long period when one policeman was left alone with the body. Thirdly, there is the strange fact that David Kelly's wife was asked to leave the house and sit in the garden when the police made a search of it for evidence. Fourthly, there is the arrival of the communication mast. And, finally, there is the US award to the chief constable.

The story cannot be told without taking account of Norman Baker's closing remark:

> 'between 1990 and his death in 2003, Dr. Kelly probably did more to make the world a more secure place than anyone else on the planet ... the honour (of a knighthood) being proposed at the time should be awarded posthumously ...'

Michael Barratt Brown

Pioneer

Harry Ratner, *A Socialist at War: In the Pioneer Corps*, Socialist Platform, ISBN 0955112796, £6.00

Harry Ratner became an active socialist at sixteen years of age, in 1936. He subsequently joined a Trotskyist group in Britain and another in France, after moving there in 1938. When the Second World War broke out, he managed to evade the German forces and get back to Britain, where he joined the Pioneer Corps. Although in theory opposed to the war, in practice he accepted 'revolutionary defencism', that is, the view that Fascism had to be fought, but the capitalist ruling classes would never do this effectively.

Annoyed that the Pioneer Corps was often ignored in official war histories, he determined to write a book to relate the history of the Corps as he knew it in the Second World War and, at the same time, to provide an account of his political activity, as a revolutionary socialist, within it.

Political consciousness within the army in the early years of the war was at a very low level. Harry declined to apply for a commission, so that he could identify with the lower ranks and seek to influence their views. As he makes clear, this was no easy task – although the establishment of the Army Bureau of Current Affairs and compulsory lectures to make the armed forces aware of the reasons why Britain was fighting improved the situation, and gave him the opportunity to put over socialist and anti-imperialist views.

When his unit landed in Italy, however, he found that few of his fellow soldiers shared his internationalist sympathies with the population as victims of fascism and war. Furthermore, as he observed with disgust in a diary that he kept at the time, former fascist officials were often allowed to retain their positions. He learnt years afterwards, with added disgust, that the Americans had made contact with the Mafia to help them take over when they landed in southern Italy.

Later in the war, Harry took part in the D-Day landings in Normandy and in the fierce fighting which ensued. Being fluent in French enabled him to ascertain the situation in the French Resistance Movement, where there was growing tension between communist elements and those loyal to General de Gaulle.

Obtaining permission to attach himself to Resistance forces advancing on Paris, where his mother and other relatives were living, he was horrified by the mob fury unleashed against former Vichy police personnel and women alleged to have slept with Germans. When he could, he intervened to stop it, but this was far from easy.

In Paris, he visited his relations and made contact with former Trotskyist comrades. After rejoining his unit, he was despatched to Belgium and agitated against the use of the Pioneers to guard coal trains against freezing and starving people trying to pilfer coal. He explained this in an article for the British Revolutionary Communist Party publication *Socialist Appeal.*

By this time, political opinion among British troops was moving to the left, but Harry only ever succeeded in recruiting one soldier to the Revolutionary Communist Party. His efforts undoubtedly aided the leftward trend in the forces, which resulted in the huge swing to Labour in the 1945 General Election. However, he now recognises that his hopes of winning large numbers over to revolutionary socialism were wildly over-optimistic.

In a previous book, *Reluctant Revolutionary*, (Socialist Platform, 1994; ISBN 0-9508423-97), Harry has already provided a fascinating account of his life as a Trotskyist militant. This new book provides greater detail and a down-to-earth account of the realities of seeking to propagate left wing socialist ideas among soldiers during the Second World War, and the risks entailed.

Today, having long ceased to be a Trotskyist, Harry is pessimistic about any possibility of an early breakthrough for genuine socialist ideas and is contemptuous of never-ending splits among those who claim to be revolutionary socialists.

His book, however, is the record of the experiences of an honest and dedicated socialist in the armed forces. Those who genuinely wish to understand the true nature of the struggle for socialism, and the practical difficulties of winning mass support, should read this excellent book.

Stan Newens

Criminal Folly

Francis Beckett, *The Great City Academy Fraud*, Continuum, 307 pages, ISBN 9780826495136, £16.99

If any British Government had proposed the following scenario for the country's educational system, one might have expected it to be rejected with contumely and derision – invite a number of rich businessmen and churchmen to put up a few thousand pounds each to become the sponsors and, in effect, the owners and managers of schools in English cities where some children are seriously deprived; close down or reduce funding for the existing schools in the area; pour millions of pounds of public money into the capital costs and all the running costs of these new schools far above the average; relax for these schools the laws about religious instruction, pupil exclusions and admissions, including children with special needs; end the rights of parents and staff; wrap it all up in a funding agreement between the sponsor and central government that cannot be challenged in law; call the schools 'academies' with some kind of educational specialism, generally something called 'business enterprise'; and top the package up with the promise of a knighthood or peerage for the sponsor.

It sounds ridiculous, criminal folly. Yet it is what has happened and is happening to about one hundred mainly secondary schools in England, not yet in Wales and Scotland. Some are avowedly faith schools, some even placing their faith in creationism. All are almost entirely financed out of taxpayers' funds, yet with no accountability to central or local elected government. On what possible argument can such a proposal have been justified? The answer is pure dogma – the belief that private provision is always superior to public, more efficient, better value for the money. The facts, apart from the spin, as they are revealed in the reports of the Office for Standards in Education (OFSTED) do not support the belief. In spite of the extra funding available to them, the academies do not perform better than other schools, and sometimes markedly less well even than those they replaced in their area.

The journalist (*New Statesman* and *Guardian*) and Prime Ministerial biographer, Francis Beckett, has written a carefully researched little book, giving the history of the 'academies' and their predecessors, the Tories 'City Technology Colleges', deemed a failure in 1991 by Labour and Tory ministers alike, but revived again in March 2000 by David Blunkett with their even more prestigious title. Sponsorship was the thing with the promise of private initiative in the management. Ironically, several of the new academies promptly removed themselves from financial contracts with the Government's Private Finance Initiative, so as to be free of the heavy long-term debt obligations involved. They were to be truly free to make their money as they saw best, choosing their own building design, including, if they wanted, a mock stock exchange, or special sports facilities, their own head and staff, and curriculum.

How come there has been no protest – from parents, teachers or local authorities? Of course there have been protests, but these have soon died down when the protesters discovered that, without the academy, there would be no alternative for the parents, no money for an old school, no new school for the children, no jobs for the staff. Central Government can, in effect, dictate without fear of local riposte. Only a national campaign could end this crime, but some localities could make a start. The following are the local authorities with one or more academies existing or in development: Barnet, Bermondsey, Bexley, Blackburn, Bradford, Brent, Bristol (2), Brighton & Hove, Croydon (2), Derby, Doncaster, Dulwich East, Ealing (2), Enfield, Gloucestershire South, Greenwich, Hackney (2), Haringey, Hillingdon, Herefordshire, Islington, Kent (4) Kensington, Kingston upon Hull, Lambeth, Leeds, Leicester, Lewisham (2), Lincolnshire North-East (2), Liverpool (2), Luton,(2), Manchester(2), Merton (2), Middlesborough (2), Milton Keynes, Northampton, Northamptonshire, Northumberland (2), Nottingham (2), Oxfordshire, Peterborough, Reading, Rochdale, Salford,(2), Sandwell (3), Sheffield (2), Slough, Solihull, Southwark (3), Staffordshire, Stockport, Sunderland (2), Telford, Walsall, Waltham Forest, Wandsworth, Westminster(2).

It is clear at a first glance that many of these are not areas of deprivation where extra funding might have been justified, and the detailed studies by Beckett show that they were not, in most cases, required to replace schools that were failing.   *MBB*